'68

'68

PACO IGNACIO TAIBO II

Translated from the Spanish
by Donald Nicholson-Smith

SEVEN STORIES PRESS
New York • London • Melbourne • Toronto

A first version of the present work, significantly shorter, entitled "Fantasmas nuestros de cada día" (Our Everyday Ghosts), appeared under the imprint of the now defunct publishing house Marco Polo, as well as in the Monterrey daily *El Porvenir* and in the magazines *Encuentro* (Mexico City) and *Casa de Las Américas* (Havana).

The translator extends many, many thanks to Alejandro, Howie, Jill, Jim, Mia, and Ramor.

First published in 1991 by Editorial Joaquín Mortiz, Mexico City
Copyright © 1991 by Francisco Ignacio Taibo Mahojo
English translation copyright © 2004 by Donald Nicholson-Smith

A Seven Stories Press First Edition.

Seven Stories Press, 140 Watts Street, New York, NY 10013; www.sevenstories.com

In Canada: Publishers Group Canada, 250A Carlton Street, Toronto, ON M5A 2L1

In the U.K.: Turnaround Publisher Services Ltd., Unit 3, Olympia Trading Estate, Coburg Road, Wood Green, London N22 6TZ

In Australia: Palgrave Macmillan, 627 Chapel Street, South Yarra VIC 3141

College professors may order examination copies of Seven Stories Press titles for a free six-month trial period. To order, visit www.sevenstories.com/textbook/, or fax on school letterhead to 212.226.1411.

Library of Congress Cataloging-in-Publication Data
Taibo, Paco Ignacio, 1949-
  [68. English]
  '68 / Paco Ignacio Taibo II ; translated by Donald Nicholson-Smith.-- A Seven Stories Press 1st ed.
    p. cm.
  Translated from Spanish.
  "A first version of the present work, significantly shorter, entitled Fantasmas nuestros de cada día (Our everyday ghosts), appeared under the imprint of the now defunct publishing house Marco Polo ..."--T.p. verso.
  ISBN 1-58322-608-7 (pbk. : alk. paper)
  1. Student movements--Mexico--History--20th century. I. Title: 1968. II. Title: Sixty-eight. III. Taibo, Paco Ignacio, 1949- Fantasmas nuestros de cada día. IV. Title.
LA428.7.T35313 2004
  378.1'981--dc20   2004003569

9 8 7 6 5 4 3 2 1

Printed in Canada.

This book, which I am never going to get right, is for my very close friend Guillermo Fernández, because without a doubt his memory is better than mine; it is also for Óscar Moreno, whose memory must have been loaned to him, because on the day that the tanks rolled into Ciudad Universitaria he had not yet been born.

The Spanish poet Ángel González wrote: "Another time will come that is unlike this one/and someone will say/you should have told other stories." During the '68 Movement, these words were faithfully inscribed on the door of a ground-floor classroom of the Political Sciences department. For years after I wondered if there were any stories left to tell."

Wherein It Is Explained That with Stuff Like This I Could Never Write a Novel

In December 1968 I began taking notes on what we had lived through. I did not trust my memory. I was wrong not to.

Over the next twenty years I proved incapable of turning the contents of those three notebooks into a novel; on the other hand, I never fell victim to amnesia. After twenty years—and here you can bring in Dumas and his three musketeers or Carlos Gardel and his "twenty years is nothing"—after twenty years, the *only* thing that works is memory. Collective memory, but also even the tiniest, most insignificant memory of a personal kind. I suspect, in fact, that the one can barely survive without the other, that legend cannot be constructed without anecdote. That there are no countries without fairy tales lurking in their shadows.

Today the Movement of '68 is one more Mexican ghost

among many unassimilated and ever-wakeful ghosts that haunt our land. It could be that because of its youth this particular ghost is still alive and well and comes automatically to the aid of our generation whenever called upon. The Saint Francis of Assisi of our doubts, Saint Che Guevara of our emotions, Saint Philip Marlowe of our private investigations, Saint Jane Fonda of our anxieties. Sixty-eight seems not only to have ensconced itself in the nostalgia factory within our minds, sharing a place there and striking the same chords as Leonard Cohen and the poems of Blas de Otero, but also to have produced the epic quantities of fuel needed to power twenty years of resistance. It has stiffened our spines in a land of submission and a hundred times placed in our mouths the words, "No! And fuck it!" It has nourished us during countless stints of unemployment, helped us wander the world selling our labor power and the smallest possible fraction of our souls, protected us from the temptations of power, and kept us away from the poisoned kiss of the Mexican State. At the very least, it has supplied us with a useful, indeed an indispensable measuring-rod for our sense of pride and guilt.

If we are all characters in a novel written on a lousy Olivetti with no ribbon, forever trying to be loyal to a personality that we once invented for ourselves, there can be no doubt that our model was forged in '68, that its finest features (the arm upstretched in a muscle-wrenching salute, the taking to the street despite paralyzing fear, the ability to live in a collective way, the desire never to sleep) were constructed then, and that ever since we have followed that model with varying degrees of success.

But getting back to the notebooks . . . My grandmother always said that you had to change your underwear every day, because if you were ever hit by a car, it would be so embarrassing, what if anyone saw, and so on. Her logic escaped me as an adolescent. Nevertheless, in 1969 I filled those three fat books with notes on the Movement, thinking that if I didn't put everything down on paper it might disappear. The notes were meant as raw material for a novel. But it didn't work out that way. Not then, not ten years later, not now. I returned to the notebooks many times, eyeing them with an odd feeling of decorum, with the same feeling my grandmother had about clean underwear. They were there in case you had an accident.

I tell myself: If I die in an airplane crash, my daughter has to find them, but it mustn't have to be easy for her. She'll find them if she makes an effort, if she roots laboriously through the piles and piles of papers that I'm going to leave her. They'll be there, but well hidden.

I never was able to write that novel. It's probably a novel that does not want to be written.

How from the Beginning This Story
Brims with Questions

How was the magic worked? What fed the bonfire? Where did they come from, the three hundred thousand students that came to the Zócalo on the day of the Great Silent Demonstration? Who gave the paraffin test to the outstretched hand? What became of Lourdes? Who was behind the door of Preparatory 1 on the day of the bazookas? How does a generation manufacture its myths? What was the menu in the Political Sciences cafeteria? What was the '68 Movement protesting? Where did the Juárez-Loreto bus start its run every morning? Who was on the right and who was on the left in September 1968? Who were the radicals and who the mensheviks? How is it that the names of deserters and suicides returned, cloaked in rumor? What poem was heard over the loudspeakers when the tanks came in? Where did the idea of *brigadismo* spring from?

How did Fanny fall in love with a cop? And when did Toño arrive at Topilejo? Where do victory and defeat begin and end? Who put up the poster of the Ginza district by night? When is revolution not revolution but reform? Why did Vocational School 5 always have the best coffee? Where was the point of no return? How did you stage a flash rally that blocked an intersection? Why were fliers hidden in the brown-paper bags bread comes in? What was the National Strike Council? Why was Romeo busted on account of a miniskirt? Where did they throw our dead? Where did they toss our dead? Where, for fuck's sake, did they throw our dead?

Loves That Last

I confess to being in love with my debt to those four months of madness in that magical year. But I confess, too, with difficulty, painfully, that the fantasy is beginning to lose its materiality, its clear outline. Transforming into myth, into a mere collection of intransigencies. I've come across some people who go so far as to say that none of it ever happened. Some say they weren't there, that they were other people then. To me that's bullshit: the fact is we were ourselves, even if we were different. Living then did not mean remembering. Living then was easier.

It is so hard for me to answer my own questions, let alone the questions of others who remember a '68 Movement that they never experienced themselves, because they were only five at the time, or because they hadn't been born, or because they were far away. All those for whom, from that time until now, I have been writing.

In 1986 I felt the power of our ghosts when the marvelous troops of the University Student Council (CEU) took to the streets. Hesitantly, I searched, from my strategic generational position on the sidewalk, for the contingent that would sweep me along with them in empathy; naturally, I ended up marching with the kids from one of the Science and Humanities Colleges, their tattered sneakers and festive spirit tied to the conviction that life should not be lived at a snail's pace. It was here that I put my ghosts to the test. If my memories of '68 were no more than points of comparison, then everything had gone to hell: I was an old fart not fit to walk alongside these new plebs. But if my memories combined seamlessly with their experiences, and with what Elena Garro called recollections of things to come, then all was not hopelessly lost.

A long-haired and near-sighted student recognized me, placed the tip of his index finger on the third button of my shirt, and told me that I had to write this book because my memories were not my private property—that there are loves that last, even for those who have not lived them in the first place.

Why Che and Bob Dylan Were Important for Some but Not for All

Part of the student generation that created the '68 Movement—a small part, no more than seven or eight thousand out of half a million high-school and college students—had come of age in a politico-cultural stew that had the virtue of universality. The madness that stalked us at life's every turn was a global madness. It had to do with our reading matter, with our heroes, myths, and refusals, with cinema, with theater, with love, and with our sources of information. We lived in thrall to the magic of the Cuban revolution and the Vietnamese resistance.

It was "El Che" who had pronounced the first words—and the last. From *Episodes of the Revolutionary War* to *Socialism and Man in Cuba*, he had guided us, led us by the hand into an ethical debate whose terms we understood perfectly. Che's death in 1967 left a void that not even his *Bolivian Diary* could fill. He was our number-one ghost. He was no more, yet he was with us still—the voice, the personality, the rousing injunction to throw everything aside and go on the road, the mocking dialogue, the project, the photograph looking down at you from every corner, the ever-growing and seemingly endless stream of fact and anecdote, the only context in which corny expressions like "total commitment" no longer seemed laughable. But above all, Che was the guy who was everywhere even though he was dead. He was dead—but he belonged to us.

We read Howard Fast and Julius Fucik, Julio Cortázar and Mario Benedetti, John Steinbeck and Ernest Hemingway, Ray Bradbury and Jesús Díaz; we read the winners of the Casas de las Américas prize and the social novels published by Editorial Futuro. We were surprised by Carlos Fuentes's *Where the Air Is Clear;* in sharp contrast to our decontextualized readings of Lenin, here was a scientific account of the formation of the new Mexican big bourgeoisie, product of a perverse union between Sonoran generals and the sanctimonious daughters of Porfirist oligarchs or shopkeepers just off the boat from Spain. Fuentes was proof that the novel was history too. The Distrito Federal could be seen clearly only from the heights of the Nonoalco Bridge. Literature was real reality. We listened to Joan Baez and Bob Dylan, Pete Seeger and Peter, Paul and Mary—the music of the anti-Vietnam War generation; secretly, we (or at least the schmaltz-prone among us) listened to Charles Aznavour and Cuco Sánchez. (The schmaltz-besotted, including me, added

Jose Feliciano's schmaltziest boleros to the mix.) Poetry was in fashion. Anthologies of Cuban revolutionary verse and of the poetry of everyday life in anti-Franco Spain were passed from hand to hand. In the courtyards of Political Sciences there were impromptu readings of Gabriel Celaya and Nazim Hikmet, and everyone knew a poem of Efraín Huerta's and at least two of César Vallejo's by heart. Movies were part of the stew, and they meant subversion. We all wailed like Algerian women on the outdoor steps of the Cine Roble after *The Battle of Algiers*, and when *8 1/2* was screened in the University film clubs it was a victory, albeit one that left us with a good many bruises courtesy of the fascist students of MURO (Movimiento Universitario de Renovadora Orientación). We could instantly recognize—and identify with each other in recognizing—such buzz words as *dazibao,* Escambray, Camiri, and Kronstadt, and we felt that certain phrases belonged to us alone: *Dicen que la distancia es el olvido.* (They say that with distance, one forgets); "Be careful, Kemosabe"; "I came to Comala because I was told that my father lived here"; (from Juan Rulfo's *Pedro Páramo*); Tarzan's "Kreeg-ah! Bundolo, tarmangani!"; or "You know nothing of Hiroshima." We didn't watch television. If television existed, it was a sickness that other people suffered from; we were far too busy inventing life to waste time on reactionary dream factories. We swore we would never visit Disneyland, and never again read Hermann Hesse.

There were not that many of us. The left—meaning the lefty

student milieu of the Valley of Mexico—was confined to a ghetto of a dozen schools: Political Sciences, Philosophy, Economics, Architecture, Psychology, Preparatory 1, Preparatory 6, Day School 8, Sciences, Physics/Mathematics at IPN (Instituto Politécnico Nacional), and Vocational 7, along with some reconquered territories in Preparatory 3, Economics at the Poli, the University of Chapingo, and Normal Superior.

Our militancy was old-style even as we aspired to the new. We were sectarian. The enemy was powerful, alien, and far away. The State was a bookish abstraction, so it made more sense to devote ourselves to interminable disputes with our pseudo-allies—the militants of the neighboring party, the next sect along, the devotees of some parallel cult. We were utterly absorbed by ideological warfare, and we produced unreadable newspapers laden with quotations from Lenin or Mao, Trotsky or Bakunin—depending on which particular club we belonged to.

Militancy meant an unremitting succession of meetings night and day, as oppressive as the rosary of any pious village woman. In our study groups we repeated our litanies, reworked our plans of action, did precious little thinking, or started malicious rumors about couples—and we all had pseudonyms even though we knew each other's real names perfectly well. There were strict Spartacists and not-so-strict Spartacists; there were Maoists and neo-Maoists; there were at least four species of Trotskyists (among them some almost indistinguishable from votaries of the Virgin of Guadalupe, who went about laying down the tasks of the proletariat "before, during, and after the Third Thermonuclear War"); and, last but not least, there were the eternal mensheviks of the Communist Party, who haunted the "real left" and were its main enemies, who were—and this was the dread epithet, a word far more potent than the worst moral stigma—"reformists." Seen in hindsight, we were a weird bunch indeed. A dying breed of devotees to some obscure religion, we might as well have strangled over the position of a comma in the Dead Sea Scrolls as waste our energies on endless internal squabbles quite unnoticed by the society of spectators that surrounded us.

Now, however, the little world of leftist sects was being invaded by real reality—the reality of the novels of Carlos Fuentes, the stories of Valadés, the fictions of Fernando Benítez, and the novels of Martín Luis Guzmán. A university would be taken over by the army, a political prisoner would go on a hunger strike, a peasant uprising would be quelled by gunfire. Here were signs of another country, one to which we had no access but which now suddenly enveloped and dumbfounded us.

For we were not Mexicans. We dwelled in a smaller city within a vast metropolis. To the east, our enclave's border was marked by the statue of General Zaragoza, whose raised finger said to us, "Go no farther; behind me lie the lands of the real." To the north, on the Pachuca road, were the statues of the Indios Verdes; beyond them was wilderness—Apache territory. To the west, the H. Steele clock at the far end of Polanco indicated not only the time but also the border of the industrial section. To the south, the laboratories of Tlalpan signaled the other extremity of the known city. Beyond them was Milpa Alta, a Zapatista terra incognita. On the other hand, we were masters of Del Valle and Narvarte (even more so since José Agustín had reinvented them in his novels), of San Rafael and Santa María, of Condesa and Roma. Ours, too, were the ice-cream parlors of Coyoacán, the París Cinema, and Café La Habana, as well as Parque México and Juárez. To us the words *reform* and *revolution* meant only the avenues we haunted. All other neighborhoods were foreign to us: places you might pass through, but where you never lingered.

In the working-class neighboorhoods we visited on occasion (after all, the manuals we had been reading and quoting until we bored ourselves stiff decreed that it was up to the working class to make the revolution), we were strange birds who showed up, then took off after showering the factory with unreadable pamphlets that the employees of the Azcapotzalco refinery or the workers at the Vallejo or Xalostoc plants would later use for ass wipes.

In 1966 I worked for a literacy program, teaching a group of Santa Clara foundry workers. I boldly opted for literature, and instead of Leninist tracts I lent them a novel by Howard Fast (I never got it back). One day, two of them showed up to class drunk. They decided that learning to read wasn't much fun and persuaded the rest of the class to go off with them and drink *toritos*. Being less sectarian than I was, they treated. The group fell apart after that, but I retain a certain nostalgia for the chemical-laden mud of Ecatepec on rainy afternoons. Sulfurous. Really real.

We were strangers, too, in history. We did not come from the national past. We didn't know why, but for us the past was an international realm that produced novels and revolutions, not a local realm belonging to the people. We were barely aware of the railroad-workers' movement and its jailed leader Demetrio Vallejo; we had heard vaguely of Rubén Jaramillo, but we could not have told his story. We felt absolutely no connection to Morelos, Zapata, Villa, to Vincente Guerrero, Hidalgo, Leandro Valle, to Guillermo Prieto, or to Mina. They were characters from a foreign history that bored preparatory teachers, really just bureaucrats, strove to misteach us; or, at best, more street names.

Foreigners in our own country; foreigners in our own history.

We weren't the only ones. We shared the university with a twin generation, one that did watch television and loved mariachi music. That reveled in the feats performed on the soccer field by the Guadalajara Chivas and the UNAM Pumas, and read books out of obligation and as by birthright. They thought their studies were simply a stepping stone to a job, but had begun to question the attraction of leaping into a society in which there were more suicides than parachutes. A society whose doors were slamming shut. We shared with them a fondness for *torterías* (sandwich shops), a unanimous endorsement of the miniskirt, and a passion for the Beatles. We were no better than they were, though we probably thought we were at the time; we were simply different. We had not yet found each other in the only possible place where that meeting could take place: Mexico City, the most Mexican Rancho Grande of all, history past and history yet to come. For the moment, without knowing or recognizing it, we shared the country in which we had happened to be born, a country that was about to turn real right in our hands.

Where It Is Revealed That We Materialists Are Not, As Is Commonly Thought, Heavy Trucks[*]

It is generally agreed that the Movement was ignited on 26 July 1968, but as always in real history, the igniters did not know at the time what it was they were igniting. There had been straws in the wind, to be sure, a distinct restlessness among the students, but small-scale activity was still the rule, fairly traditional in form, with old-style leadership and an old-style approach to political action. Here and there something new was stirring, but it was hard to see the signs precisely because of the speed with which things were happening: the Vietnam solidarity demonstrations gave birth to *brigadismo*—mobile action groups of five or six comrades that would hold flash rallies anywhere in the city; the 1967 student strike in the technical colleges; the demonstration

---

[*] *Materialistas,* in Mexican Spanish, are heavy-goods vehicles.—Translator.

against the Hanoi bombings, when doves were released from garbage cans all over the Zona Rosa to blow the minds of the riot police guarding the gringo embassy; Demetrio Vallejo's hunger strikes in support of freedom for political prisoners, and the parallel hunger strike it sparked at Political Sciences.

Come 26 July we Reds went into the street, about seven or eight thousand of us, perhaps a few hundred more than a month earlier at a demonstration in solidarity with the Cuban revolution that extended down San Juan de Letrán. A more or less routine left-wing demonstration. The usual.

I marched with Santiago Ramírez and a couple of guys who said they were Costa Ricans, though years later I found out they were part of what would become the Sandinista movement. Foreign elements even more foreign than us, they had pegged us as potential guides.

When the demonstration rounded the corner onto La Alameda, we could hear the chanting of other groups some distance away. Whether because Santiago and I had New Left leanings and were less orthodox than most, or because he was the son of a psychologist and I of a journalist, we left our demonstration, whose climax of soporific speeches could easily be foreseen, and joined the bystanders on the sidewalk. We covered ten or more blocks with the *ticos*, the supposed Costa Ricans, following along behind. We quickly found ourselves in the midst of a march of Poli students protesting the progovernment groups on their campus and attacks by youth gangs. They were heading down toward the Zócalo and heaping shit on the National Front of Technical Students (FNET)— a government-supported student organization used to maintain discipline at the Poli—as they went. They seemed much more convivial than us, considerably less uptight. More genuinely pissed off. More innocent.

All at once, the metal shutters of the stores along the street began to come down. From the head of the march came shouts and the *paff, paff* of exploding tear-gas canisters. Seconds later we were surrounded by riot police who, giving no order to disperse, set about beating us, taking advantage of the fact that we were now trapped in the narrowness of Calle Palma. Doors were quickly shut. I clearly remember the blood flowing down the forehead of someone who came up beside me and the shoes lost by people running where there was no space to run as they strove to escape the front line. There was the feeling that you would never get out of this without getting beaten up. As the riot police closed in the crowd grew denser. You heard screams and grunts, and blows to the head delivered without mercy, indeed with hatred. The sense that there was no way out and that the beatings would be endless created panic. One of our *ticos* started to pull out a pistol, but Santiago and I stopped him: if he fired a shot, we would be massacred for sure. The riot police had guns, not just batons. They pressed in upon us, and more of us fell bleeding to the ground. By good fortune a gap appeared in the barrier of blue. We raced through the breach but fell straight into the clutches of three or four cops in a parking area not far away. I remember Santiago heroically throwing himself upon a policeman who was about to club a vocational-school kid in the head and his rolling over on the ground with the cop clutched tightly in his arms. Then we were running again, through streets in the city center that, as I recall, were unlighted. I remember reaching Preparatory 3 and breaking in on a film-society screening, jumping onto the stage, yelling for lights, and announcing that the riot police had gone mad, that the repressive government of Díaz Ordaz, etc., etc. Feeling so certain that something new was happening. The images that clung obstinately to the retina on their way to the memory. Ending the night together at the house of a friend who had just had a baby son. The news that the Cuba demo had also been put down with gas and clubs. Had they really gone crazy?

This was not the first time we had been beaten up by the cops. It was one of the Mexican state's demented customs to give the students a bit of stick every now and again, just to show them who was boss. The year before, police had assaulted Vocational School 7, and the 1965 Vietnam demo had been broken up with batons, wounding fifty people. I was one of them, earning myself a three-inch gash over the left eyebrow, where a plainclothesman slugged me with a metal bar rolled up in a newspaper. In Sonora, too, the year before, the army had been sent in, and all of us had heard stories of what had occurred two years earlier at Morelia University. All the same, this was different: what were they cooking up now?

In the meantime, we ended that night at a christening, summing up with difficulty the events of the day but happy to find ourselves still in one piece. We showed each other our cuts and bruises. Fear, for now, was gone.

A Weekend When Everything Began

Could the government see further than us? Did they anticipate the emergence of a vast student movement, and were they out to strangle it in its infancy? Was one faction of the government using this as a stick with which to beat another in the presidential race? We had, ourselves, spoken of something known as "the Movement." And we had seen signs that such a thing might exist, but this would be confirmed in our minds only if they— the invisible enemy—believed in it too. The May events in France had made headlines in all the papers, as had the Prague Spring, the student mobilization in Brazil, the occupation of Columbia University in New York, and the Córdoba uprising in Argentina. Did these idiots really think that some sort of international contagion was at work? Could they believe in the virus that we believed in (sort of)? Unlikely. This was Mexico, gentlemen. It would never go that far here.

The next day we found out from the box and the papers that one of Mexico's many secret-police agencies had raided the Communist Party's headquarters overnight and arrested several Communist student leaders visiting the editorial offices of the party's daily. A few hours earlier there had been a roundup of foreigners, most of them onlookers picked up on the fringes of demonstrations because they looked like hippie or student types—quite consistent, of course, with the hallowed Mexican political and police custom of rounding up a few aliens as proof of an international plot.

The ball was rolling—and rolling into the most unlikely places. We still didn't know what the Movement was, but it was growing. In the student quarter in the center of the city a strange spontaneous mobilization now began: students from the preparatory schools ringed the area, stopping trucks and confronting the riot police, who were eager to bust some more heads. The more politicized IPN schools began the day with assemblies, demanding the abolition of the FNET and the release of those arrested. It was Saturday, and the University was quiet. All weekend long the skirmishing in the city center continued, which must have made the mafiosi in the Palacio Nacional a little antsy: the new Vandals were a bit too close for comfort. Meanwhile, the old commie left met in their boy-scout club rooms to consider sixteen-point agendas on which the new movement probably occupied the third or fourth place, somewhere below the usual threats of expulsion for nonpayment of dues.

The Shattered Door

By Monday we were on strike. Initiated in some of the IPN schools, the strike was total and simultaneous within the humanities wing of UNAM—the National Autonomous University of Mexico—in the wake of enormous rallies. And it was effectively total in the preparatory schools in the center of the city, which were surrounded by police. Slowly but surely, it was gaining ground. So close were developments to a text of Trotsky's that we could barely believe it:

> It seemed as though the strike had wanted to make a few random experiments, only to abandon them in short order and move on; but that was merely the appearance. In reality the strike was about to unfurl to its fullest extent. . . . The strike takes charge of the situation and, feeling itself to be on firm ground, annuls all

decisions taken hitherto in a spirit of moderation. . . .
As the number of strikers grows, the strike gains in con-
fidence.

The various schools met in assemblies, voted to strike, and
organized marches within the precincts of the University to
bring the strike to other departments. The decisive argument
was invariably the appeal to unanimity: if others are on strike,
why shouldn't we be, too? Science was striking, Orthodontics
also, Engineering was on board, as was Chemistry.

At Political Sciences we waited on nobody. We had been on
strike for a week already, demanding the release of political prisoners. So far from trying to get in step with the Movement, we
felt we *were* the Movement. Spectators at this hour of truth, we
were disconcerted by the idea that our little strike would no
longer be the only one: was the role of the vanguard to shine
like a beacon in the depths, or wasn't it? The School of
Agriculture joined the stoppage, and the Normal School students backed them up. Skirmishing continued in the city center, with clashes between students and riot police. Rumor and
the information brigades that ventured outside the Ciudad
Universitaria, the UNAM campus, in search of contacts, told of
burning buses and brickbat wars, of policemen stabbed and students savagely clubbed.

On Tuesday, blinded by their overweening arrogance, the
authorities launched the army against Preparatory 1. The

school's entrance, dating to colonial times, was struck by bazooka fire; there was shooting, and hundreds of arrests. A group of students took refuge on the roof as the soldiers, with bayonets fixed, entered the courtyards of their school, where there are murals by Orozco, Revueltas, Siqueiros, and Rivera. For a time everything took on symbolic force. They had blasted the historic doorway of the preparatory to pieces. With bazookas. The famous door. But then we were beyond symbolism, thanks to the photos, which showed blood pooled amid the splintered wood.

Meanwhile, a program was being drawn up that addressed issues arising from the situation while also incorporating the demands of the most radical sector: free political prisoners, abolish the riot police, dismiss the police chiefs. In the University a council of representatives of the striking departments began meeting. We were now governed by a Stakhanovite inner clock: the mimeograph machines worked overtime. The paper stores of the university press and the department of social services were duly raided; propaganda brigades started collecting money in the street and on city buses. The Movement was being born, and it used the most advanced forms of action learned over the preceding months.

The press was lying: the door of Preparatory 1 had not been destroyed by bazooka fire but by Molotov cocktails thrown by the students themselves; those clubbed to death had not been clubbed, they had died from eating a tainted cheese sandwich, a *torta de queso,* hours earlier; the student assemblies were organized by provocateurs . . . We couldn't have cared less: they lied because that was who they were, and their lies strengthened our convictions. For our part we knew the truth; we got our news by word of mouth. Eyewitness accounts were told and retold: everything had been seen by someone, heard by someone, and was recounted by everybody.

In the university assemblies a few liberal professors got to their feet, and for the first time we heard the provocation theory, according to which we ought to demobilize because we were the victims of a gigantic provocation: the State was manipulating us. But shit! Those dead were our dead. We were the ones who had been clubbed. The real provocation was the call to demobilize. So—long live the strike!

We didn't care about "the beautiful colonial doorway of San Ildefonso." What we cared about was the blood visible in the photos behind the destroyed door; what we cared about was the disappearance of the bodies. We had plunged head first into the land of the real. Almost a thousand people had been arrested. Who were they? In the first place there were members of the Communist Party, seized in all innocence, and then there were the anonymous (and hence presumably unpoliticized) Poli and preparatory students who had taken the brunt of the first clashes. The future cadres of the Movement were as yet untouched, busy with the organizational tasks of a tidal wave that just kept growing and growing. The more conservative schools joined the strike one after another; the government's cheering section in the University, the *porristas,* were routed and isolated; and the PRI vanished from the departments, rubbed out by an immense eraser that obliterated everything. We painted graffiti on the doors of the lecture halls, the fences, the windows, the buses— even the roofs of the school buildings to send a message to the police helicopters.

It was mindblowing. Bazookas or no bazookas, we learned from the information brigades that the clashes were continuing in the city center. The prime movers were the younger students of the vocational and preparatory schools: the "others," the ones who a week ago had never read a page of Lenin, and who now, swept into the whirlpool, would not need to. Others—but just like us.

One brigade of left-wing militants from the Department of Sciences found itself surrounded by a group of vocational students who had learned to pelt the riot police with stones using slingshots, then take refuge in the courtyards of their school. The militants taught the vocational students how to produce fliers and organize propaganda brigades. And the militants in turn learned that even bricks need to be aimed high and that Molotov cocktails should have very short fuses.

What was going on? For those of us who had got our politics out of books, political reality was a completely new school. All we knew was that there was a Movement and that it had to be defended against those who sought to destroy it with clubs and bazooka fire, and protected from those who wanted to suffocate it with words, slow it down, and halt it. We knew that we had to make it grow, nourish it, and take it beyond itself. The State had come into our lives as the face of evil: the president's perverse monkey features, so often caricatured, personified it perfectly. The riot police, seen dragging a bloodied student by the hair in a photograph in *¿Por Qué?,* were the immediate enemy. All those guys who lied, who kept us down, who kissed ass, who threatened us—they were the real Mexico. But then we, the new we, made from the many that we had been, decided that, fuck it, we were also the real Mexico.

Concerning a Reorganization of Life and a Reduction of Sleeping Hours for Want of One's Usual Bed

Because it was carpeted, the anteroom to the director's office became the first dormitory for our striking department. Alejandro Licona opened the door with a karate chop. The laws of 1968 were replacing the laws of the University. We put padlocks on the file cabinets.

As he was bound to, Alejandro would eventually become an unforgettable character for me. He was ugly and wore the thick glasses of the myopic; tall and scrawny, he was the department's official and ever-amazing pick-up artist, the one who made out with the summer-school gringas. Which was no doubt why he was sent by the strike committee to tour North American universities and publicize our struggle and collect funds. Every now and then he would call the tapped department phones to recount solidarity meetings in schools with such exotic names as New York or Kansas, Chicago or California. His return to Mexico, halfway through the Movement, was even more spectacular. He was picked up by government agents at the airport carrying a couple of black briefcases stuffed with dollars, the haul from his collecting in the gringo colleges. He was unshaven, red eyed from lack of sleep. They placed him under guard in a private room and spent half an hour threatening him with death. But he escaped from his captors and led them on a wild chase through the corridors of the airport. Eventually he ran into a brigade out on propaganda duty, who bundled him into a car and deposited him with us at Political Sciences. His tale was so incredible that we all believed him.

Anyway, as I was saying, it was Alejandro who broke open the door and opened up the space that would be transformed into a mixed dormitory—a rather puritanical one, to be sure, with nothing going bump in the night. We would stretch out in two rows, fifteen or so jokers in each, toe to toe, and wait for someone from the Dormitory Organizing Committee to cover the whole lot of us with one immense velvet curtain. As for pillows, we had our jackets. The lights were never turned off: there was always someone who would rather read than sleep.

By far the most exciting part was night-guard duty—what we called rounds. The wee hours were a truly crazy time. On one of the first nights we decided to put this dead time to good use by decorating the department. We tied the place up in an enormous bow of two-color typewriter ribbon, more than four hundred meters of it; the two colors, of course, were red and black—the colors of the strike. On another sleepless night, Manuel El Chiquito, Trobamala, and I set about painting the Sciences tower red and black. And I remember that on the third night of the strike we decided to pay a visit to the comrades of Orthodontics to serenade them in the spirit of solidarity. We figured that they were new to the craziness of the revolution and that they deserved something like this from us old hands at Political Sciences.

The days were more reasonable.

Confetti

On 31 July we went into the street in massive numbers. The government had relinquished some of the schools taken over by the authorities earlier, but it had also mounted new assaults on others, among them the National Theater School. In their frenzy the authorities had used police dogs to attack the students.

The demonstration was led off the campus by the rector of the University, its main demand being the defense of the autonomy of the academy. Some of us wanted more than that. On a rainy afternoon a hundred thousand students flowed into the street from the esplanade of the Ciudad Universitaria. They aimed to go no further than Félix Cuevas, beyond which were dragons. Dozens of armored vehicles, squads of police, battalions of riot police, military transports, and soldiers with fixed bayonets had been deployed. The Zócalo was off-limits to us. But we were very many, thousands upon thousands, and we spoke with one voice.

The high point of the day came when we passed the housing projects, and confetti rained down upon us courtesy of the tenants. We all gazed up as the blizzard of colored paper descended. We were not alone.

That same evening President Díaz Ordaz, in a speech from the city of Guadalajara, tendered his famous "outstretched hand" to the students in exchange for their submission. An outstretched hand—if you apologize. The imaginative riposte appeared the next day on thousands of handbills and flyposters: *A la mano tendida, la prueba de la parafina* (Give the outstretched hand the paraffin test). I think this slogan was the brainchild of Jaime Goded, mastermind of student propaganda and leader of the Marilyn Monroe Brigade. I remember that we celebrated his inspiration in a rather odd way: by going with a whole truckful of *brigadistas*, complete with banners, pamphlets, and megaphones, to see Jaime's newborn daughter at an apartment in the Florida section. By the time Evelyn was halfway across the sidewalk, holding her baby up for us to see, we had calmed down a bit, and we applauded enthusiastically. The baby was so diminutive, so wrinkled. A grinning Jaime showed her off. Then the brigade went to demonstrate in the markets in the south of the city.

Of Women and Mattresses

Jaime's daughter would grow up in a worse world. Very soon her father would be in prison. But to be a woman in '68 was no bad thing. For thousands of sisters the times offered a chance to be equal. Sixty-eight antedated the new feminism. It was better than feminism. It was violently egalitarian—and if it wasn't always, it always could be. One man, one woman, one vote—and one collection box, one stack of fliers, one level of risk . . . That it mattered little whether you wore a skirt or pants was a given. Being a man then was better too, because those women existed.

They were great. And gorgeous, really gorgeous. They wore their undeniable beauty without fuss—and without makeup. Any role model worth the name was supposed to be cinematographic, but in those days Anita Ekberg and Sophia Loren, even Kim Novak's honeyed glances and Elke Sommer's poutiness, had ceased to operate. The sixties generated its own points of reference at more than twenty-four frames per second: miniskirts, a well-thumbed Simone de Beauvoir novel dangling from the hand, fishnet stockings, velvet hairbands, ponytails, bangs, plaid skirts, boots with blue jeans, and candlelight dinners with white wine and smoked ham. I have been stuck in that moment every single day since. I was certainly there when, three years later, I met Paloma. And I think I am still there when I watch my sixteen-year-old daughter brushing her hair in these distant nineties.

What fucking apron-wearing wusses we were! We couldn't eat a taco at a taco stand. We had never danced at a housing-project dance—that came later. As for me, ever the late arrival, I never liked Tecate with lime and tequila. We had no sense of humor and no sense of savoir-faire in so many areas of life. Not one of us was capable of speaking up for chocolate malteds or quesadillas in the doorway of the bakery. Maybe it was the women who first defended such things even as they discoursed on Vargas Llosa's "The Cubs": they had a better sense of everyday life and were so much less limited than we were.

They could also laugh, and get you to laugh with them, at any moron who announced, say, that "the sisters obviously can't go out painting slogans at night." We were so damn equal—and so damn different. Sure enough, there was always some dope who wanted the women to run the kitchen of the department café; but there would always be someone slightly less dopey to say that that was everybody's job.

The women had family stories, recounted with fury, about horrendous struggles for equality; as often as not they had a black-and-blue arm to prove what they said. They told of fights over an extra half-hour outside, over the right to be in the city at night, over the disastrous discovery of a pack of birth-control pills. Only by resorting to screams and threats of leaving home did they hold their own against unyielding mothers, retrograde grandparents, and pro-PRI fathers. But, Televisa notwithstanding, the stereotypical Mexican "little mother" was on her way out.

According to the myth, the sixties happened largely on beds: big round beds, hammocks, mattresses on the floor, straw mats, you name it. Rock'n'roll, marijuana, and sex. Rock? Well, yes. Marijuana? For the most part, marijuana was what the cops liked to plant on you. And sex? In Mexico sexual liberation was not a high-profile arrival, save perhaps in the spiel of inveterate Casanovas. No, sex seemed to be experienced as part of a sweet and fairly romantic and egalitarian project, a project framed in the literature stacks, in Guevarism, even in obscure traces ferried by our chromosomes from Gutiérrez Nájera or Amado Nervo. The myth says there was a lot of action in 1968. A lot less, I'd say, than in 1967, and even less than in 1966. In '68 there was, well, less time.

People always say that there was more sex back then, before, that there is more somewhere else, at some other time, across the street, in the next tribe, in Sweden. . . But I suppose the

Swedes say the same thing about us, and that those from way-back-when say it about the people we were then, just as the people we are now are liable to say it about those growing up now.

And Sometimes We Believe in the Informative Value of Tremors Running Through the Atmosphere

A movement results from combinations that even its own participants cannot control. And that its enemies cannot calculate. It evolves in ways that cannot be predicted, and even those who foresee it are taken by surprise.

It was raining during those days, and the city had turned enormous. I wanted to capture the moment in a poem but could not. Happily, there were others who could, others who had written earlier, in other cities under the rain. Like the sometimes pedestrian Yucatán poet José Peón Contreras (to us, at the time, the name of an avenue), who had asked: "Where can the beach be that awaits us?"

Since I couldn't manage a poem, I crisscrossed the city from appointment to appointment, rally to minimarch, assembly to conference, *brigadista* powwow to underground planning session. I went from setting up a mimeograph machine to stealing paper, from a siesta snatched in some truck to hair-raising trips in Galileo, which was Paco Pérez Arce's car, and on to a rendezvous with a bunch of refinery workers in Puente de Vigas. From there to a *quince años* party in Doctores, where with waltz music in the background we planned a propaganda campaign in the factories of Ixtapalapa, or else to Mixcoac to eat chicken soup as the day broke. Sitting still was a sin—the only sin I can remember from those days. I spent my time picking up the vibes, which I would discuss later with my two ideological gurus, Armando Bartra and Martín Reyes, both in their undershirts, cooped up in an apartment in Lomas de Plateros so full of smoke from the Del Prado plant that you could barely see the walls.

There was no day or night, just actions, the street, and vibrations that called for interpretation by someone.

The Godchildren

At the beginning of August, with the strike underway, the student center-left and left-left published their list of demands, solidifying the loose patchwork of demands and thus getting a jump on the authorities, who were striving to confine the conflict to the University and to a very liberal defense of academic freedom. The student program was very brief, consisting famously of six points that resounded throughout the country thanks to the voices of thousands of *brigadistas* clinging to lampposts and passing out millions of handbills: freedom for political prisoners; repeal of the law against "social dissipation," which was used to justify the jailing of political dissidents; dismissal of the police leadership; apportionment of blame for repressive measures; compensation for the wounded and for the families of those killed; and abolition of the riot police. This set of demands had a second meaning, too, understood by all and taken to heart by all, namely, the call for democracy. The right of citizens to live in society was being won in the streets and imposed upon a repressive power structure.

On 5 August the first consolidated demonstration of the new Movement was a march from Zacatenco to the Santo Tomás campus of the IPN, and it signaled the political rout of the gangsterism of the FNET, the conservatism of the heads of the IPN schools, and the vacillating liberals. It also signaled a victory over fear.

At the march's halfway point many people left their contingents and contemplated from the sidelines the demonstration of which they had been part until a few seconds before. What they saw was how very, very many we were. Each school made its individual presence felt, chanting its own slogans and carrying its own enormous banner at the head of its contingent, so that no one could forget that they had not failed to make it, that they had answered the call, that they were well and truly there. The Movement might be anonymous, but the basis of its unity was clear: the school, "*el cole.*"

Memory tends to simplify, whether by retaining absurdly trivial anecdotes or by seeing the big picture strictly in black and white. The Movement was, in fact, many things at once. For thousands of students, it meant an unmasking of the Mexican state as an emperor with no clothes. It meant the occupation of schools and the creation of libertarian common spaces based on assemblies. It meant family discussions in thousands of homes. It meant crisis for the traditional ways of misinforming the nation, a confrontation with leafleting, with the live voice, and with the rescuing power of rumor as alternatives to a controlled press and television. It also meant violence, repression, fear, prison, assassination. But above all, far more than anything else, it meant the reengagement of a generation of students with their own society, their investment in neighborhoods hitherto unknown to them, discussions on the bus, a breaking-down of barriers, the discovery of solidarity among the people, and, as they made it past the gray perimeter of the factories and reached those who were to be found within, the closest encounter yet with a mass of "others."

If the deepest meaning of the Movement lay in what it was without knowing it, its limitations lay in its message, so student-centered, exclusive, private, egoistic: we had *our* dead, *our* victims of repression, *our* freedoms—even *our* police, which we wished to abolish. But Mexican society was full of other dead, other wounded, other police (not to mention corrupt union leaders, factory bosses, suburban caciques, and venal functionaries). There were other authoritarianisms, which this first wave of students were just beginning to recognize but which they could not yet make into their enemy. Their reason understood, but not yet their heart, as Saint-Exupéry's goody-goody would have said. We still needed time to become real Mexicans. The Movement's heart did not reach out to strangers, apart from the political prisoners. All the same, we were beginning to discern the country through the fog. You couldn't go out into the street and not be changed by it. And meanwhile the people of the Valley of Mexico, even if they were on another planet, felt sympathy for these students: these sons and daughters, neighbors, godchildren, nieces and nephews of the lady in Apartment 7, cousins of old Amalia . . . And the people of the Valley of Mexico filled the students' red-and-black collecting cans with coins and took their little leaflets—so full of pompous phrases, so rhetorical—and in the markets gave them melons and potatoes, yams and avocados (maybe a little bruised) and papayas, and they wished them well.

Menu

Menu for the Nguyen Van Troi Cafeteria, Department of Political Sciences, in early August 1968. Cooks: a Maoist, a leftist Christian democrat, a Trotskyist, two miniskirted Guevarists. To drink: *agua de Jamaica* (hibiscus flower tea). To eat: chicken soup, boiled potatoes with salt, and bananas for dessert. Menu remains unchanged for four days, until food donated by Mixcoac Market vendors is finished. No siesta. Brigade activity in Ciudad Nezahualcóyotl: newspaper distribution, factory visit, assembly. At night: massive graffiti-painting campaign. There are one hundred painting brigades in this school. Thousands of painting brigades to paint the entire humanities wing. The city as rainbow. A quick slogan: ¡HOCICÓN! (Big mouth—in reference to the supremo of the Republic). A not-so-quick slogan (because it has one letter more): ¡LIBERTAD!

We Remember the Days of Glory but Tend to Forget They Were Fourteen-Hour Days

During the mobilization of August 1968 the brigades occupied the streets without exposing a flank to the repressive forces. Those forces perceived the Movement as an unmanageable mass. With whom could you negotiate when the leadership consisted of three hundred people? Who was an interlocutor, especially an interlocutor you could frighten and corner? Who could you buy off? The Movement failed to fit any of the State's usual ways of dealing with an adversary. The mobilization had two faces: the slippery brigades on the one hand and imposing demonstrations with half a million or more participants on the other. The leadership, calling itself the National Strike Council (CNH) consisted of three representatives from each school on strike; these were often rotating delegates, which made the Council easy to infiltrate but impossible to split, scare, corrupt, or detach from its base through negotiation. Since control was denied by these means, the only options left were isolation and repression. In any event negotiation had no place in the operating procedures of an authoritarian system whose reference points were the Aztecs, Cortés, and the PRI. According to our national tradition, an authority that negotiates surrenders its power.

On the propaganda front, the government had already lost the capital and several provincial cities to which the strike had spread. Television and the printed press were almost worthless against the half-million voices that rebutted their lies day in and day out.

The first organizational allies of the student movement now joined the fray, namely the Coalition of High-School and Higher-Education Teachers and the Assembly of Intellectuals, Artists, and Writers. Here were to be found the remnants of the best of the previous generation: Carlos Félix, José Revueltas, Eli de Gortari, Luis Alberto de la Garza (my history teacher at Preparatory 1), José Agustín, Carlos Monsiváis (our future electrical expert), Armando Castillejos (the great lawyer), and the painters, who became more radical as they painted, as they registered their enduring solidarity in the most ephemeral of muralisms.

The streets were getting bigger, more comprehensive. And in our minds the feeling grew that the Movement was somehow greater than the sum of its parts. A feeling that now, twenty years later, especially in view of the elections of 1988, I admit still has life in it: the vague idea that the country could change, that we could perhaps therefore build a different country; obviously, this was a feeling that arose from our power. On 13 August we tried to lay claim to the Zócalo. The demonstration set out from the Santo Tomás campus, with Poli and UNAM contingents alternating. The call to demonstrate gave this advice: "Should it be impossible to reach the Zócalo, your contingent should scatter into the downtown area, holding flash rallies and trying to avoid clashes with the authorities." The State was falling back, however, and two hundred thousand of us marched into the Zócalo. The city was immense, the streets wide. The Zócalo is the largest public square in the world, a space that absorbed all echoes and made us cry like idiots. I remember the earnestness of the Poli nurses who almost wanted someone to collapse from dehydration just so they could leap into action. I remember the enormous banner with Che's face on it that the Philosophy contingent unfurled. And I remember the text of a letter sent from the Lecumberri prison by Víctor Rico Galán:

> "The future prospects for developing the movement you are leading lie with the workers. . . . When, during the big demonstrations that you organize, the people throw sheets of plastic or paper down to you from their windows to help you keep yourselves dry; when poor folk,

whose clothing clearly reveals their near-destitute condi-
tion, come up to you marchers to applaud, take your
leaflets, or show their sympathy by handing you bread or
fruit; when these things happen, it is because the people,
even without the guidance of its organizations, even
without the means of making its great voice heard, is
seeking opportunities to express its support. . . .
Students, hear the people!"

From the slammer, Víctor had put his finger on the new
focus of the debate that was taking place in the assemblies, in
strike-committee meetings, among *brigadistas*, and in the
National Strike Council. How far was the Movement going to
go? Time smoothes out furrows, harmonizes discrepancies,
homogenizes everything. Now it almost seems as though we
were a bloc of unanimous voices, a unified mass without dissen-
sion. But, as Marx's housekeeper and Lin Piao (who died in a
plane crash—in his kitchen!) can testify, we detested one another. No love at all was lost; small wars were legion. In the bosom
of the Movement discussion was bitter—often far more violent
than it had to be. The Movement had rid itself of infiltrators,
and the FNET, the conservative teachers, and the paternalistic
school principals had all been sent packing. The vanguard was
divided into three distinct tendencies (the differences being far
less clear among the broad mass base). In the first place, there
was a right wing, headed by the University rector, which could

count on the support of a good portion of the administrative staff, which influenced not a few UNAM and IPN teachers, and which sought to confine conflict to student-related and defensive issues. These limits, thankfully soon extended, represented the sane side of the system itself. The original demands of this tendency were a return to normal, autonomy for the University and freedom for university students taken prisoner. The attitude of the State and the turn of events meant that the right wing had the leadership role during the first week after the bazooka attack; thereafter, thanks to its mobilizing efforts and its composition, the National Strike Council took over. The Council and the teachers' coalition embraced the movement's other two clear tendencies: a center, represented by UNAM's Department of Sciences, most schools of the IPN, and several of the preparatories; and a left, represented by the Humanities schools in the Ciudad Universitaria, by Chapingo, by part of the IPN's Physics-Mathematics and Economics departments, the UNAM Architecture School, and Preparatories 6 and 8. Differences between left and center became manifest over almost any issue: the main rationale for the mobilization of brigades, whether to take Radio UNAM over completely, march routes, or the correct response to the government's first hints of willingness to negotiate. It is still very hard for me now to analyze the respective positions, for it involves disentangling them from the sectarian fantasies that enveloped them at the time. Underlying the debate was a confrontation between the

Communist Youth organization and its most recent dissidents on the one hand and all the groups to its left on the other. The attitude of the center was founded on the idea of pushing for negotiations. We on the left spoke up for a public dialogue, but we did not want any direct dialogue with Díaz Ordaz. They wanted to restrict the Movement to student action and felt the essential thing was to ensure a student victory. On the left we felt that the Movement must be carried beyond the universities and, in accordance with Rico's message from prison, brought to the people as part of a quest for something further. With the benefit of twenty years' hindsight, I daresay we were all rational (such an elusive quality) to a degree. Were we crazier than the centrists? Was the revolution, of which we spoke only in whispers, in the realm of the impossible? Could the repression to which the Movement was destined have been obviated by means of negotiating skills?

In Political Sciences and Chapingo we urged that the brigades go into industrial neighborhoods to get our message out there and, by promoting democracy for all, ensure that demonstrations yet to come would head not for the Zócalo but for Glorieta de Camarones, the center of the industrial park in the north of the Distrito Federal. Sometimes we didn't just talk about going there—we actually went there.

But things were more complicated, because the small political groups were not masters of the Movement, nor were they even masters of their own militants, transformed overnight into leaders of a mass movement answerable to its assemblies. I am tempted to forget this part of the story, the part that tells how often I screamed at Pino, now my friend, that he was a reformist prick, which gave him the chance to retort that I was an adventurist jerk.

And of course this whole debate was inextricably bound up with the necessity of responding to the government day in and day out. What about us? Did we want a victory? We surely did, but we could not define it beyond the six points . . . Meanwhile, much verbal vitriol was exchanged and countless insults covered the walls and filled our leaflets. In the end, though, we all found ourselves in the same trench with bullets really whistling through the air, because in the real Mexico the true "others"— enemies under the command of a malign president—were killing real people.

Radio Rumor

If the media's submission to the power of the government has become a suffocating reality in our modern society, in '68 it was terrifying. Radio, television, and the printed press voiced a consensus worthy of the most banana-driven of banana republics: they pushed the official version every time, cooking numbers, manipulating content and images, and voicing the opinions of some while denying a voice to others.

This was the context in which Radio Rumor was born.

Radio Rumor was a jungle telegraph of untraceable origin that effectively counteracted official sources.

It was anything but objective, but it was governed by a relative loyalty to the truth: it was partial, prone to exaggerate, alarmist, and sensationalist. And this in the most primary way, because Radio Rumor was uncontrollable.

The Movement had thousands of street orators, hoardings,

and spray-painted buses at its disposal, as well as millions of handbills and countless nightly conversations in which to propagandize family members, girlfriends or boyfriends, or neighbors—this being the outer fringe of activism. From all this emerged Radio Rumor, a territory held by everyone and no one, frequently irrational, quintessentially Mexican.

The army fired repeatedly on a student brigade at the gates of the Atzcapotzalco refinery, clashes had occurred with the workers, and before long the word on Radio Rumor was that a strike had broken out in the refinery, and cars were already lining up at all the gas stations. . .

But there were times when Radio Rumor did not exaggerate, when it was quite accurate. For example, the press reported that a student from the UNAM Business School had died after eating a tainted cheese sandwich. Radio Rumor knew that he had died of a concussion after being clubbed by a riot policeman. Radio Rumor was imprecise, vague, it didn't know the student's name or age, but on the other hand it conveyed the remarkably precise information that he had been wearing a yellow sweater.

Radio Rumor might be incoherent, absurd, disjointed, but it was on target when it retaliated and rigorous when it passed judgment.

The official account claimed that the president had been operated on for a detached retina. Radio Rumor was aware of the cause and, despite official silence on the matter, was able to inform us that it was a twenty-cent piece, thrown by some anonymous avenger amid the confetti of 16 September; it knew, even, that it was a copper twenty-cent piece, and not a five-cent piece, or a peso. Radio Rumor could be dead-on when it wanted to.

The official account said that those arrested were being held in Military Camp 1. Radio Rumor knew more: it knew that they were being tortured.

Radio Rumor waged a permanent information war with the Mexican state over statistics; figures were its favorite battleground. When the official account was that 6 schools were on strike, Radio Rumor gave the correct figure: 26 ½—the half because at Preparatory 7 the students of the afternoon session had not gone on strike. The newspapers echoed the bulletins of the interior ministry, which said that 70,000 students had gone on strike. Radio Rumor gave the correct figure: 500,000.

In the absence of reliable information from other sources, Radio Rumor hyped and invented: on the day of the bazooka attack, it dreamed up a coup d'état, despite the objections of those of us who pointed out that a palace coup had been a fait accompli since the beginning of the Díaz Ordaz presidential term.

Radio Rumor favored items of secondary importance but always showed a keen sense of drama. At times you felt it must come from the same people who brought us photo-novels. We learned exactly what breed of dog accompanied the riot police and bit students during their eviction from the National

Theater School, but we never found out the number of the military unit that mounted the assault with fixed bayonets.

Only Radio Rumor knew about the killings in Tlatelolco, telling us that the dead had been laid out in a hangar in the military part of the airport, telling us, too, of the flight over the Gulf of Mexico from which the bodies of murdered students were tossed into the sea. Only Radio Rumor counted the victims and gave them names—the beginning of real resistance to forgetfulness.

When Maricarmen Fernández Grabbed My Ass

A bus from the Juárez-Loreto route started showing up in the department parking lot. The driver would arrive at seven in the morning, knock on the door of one of the lecture rooms, and ask us to paint slogans on his vehicle, then he would go off on his regular run through the Distrito Federal. Normally, buses would get painted up by brigades all over the city and would proudly broadcast our message until the forces of the enemy, in the shape of the sanitation teams of the Distrito Federal, took them off for un-painting. The Juárez-Loreto driver didn't want to waste all that time, nor did he care to run the risk of running into a group of *brigadistas*, so he came early to get his bus painted. That way he could also suggest slogans and take part in the decorating. On the third day of this we decided to enlist him. It was agreed that his story, if we were stopped, would be that we had commandeered his bus. Then we organized the first monster brigade: thirty students with a big pile of red flags, two megaphones, and a guitar began to make incursions into the industrial areas of the city. Once we went into the General Motors plant, to the stupefaction of the police guarding the gates, who didn't risk stopping us. We filed through the inner courtyards singing, went into the workshops and held flash rallies and handed out fliers even in the manager's office. But this kind of thing remained an isolated phenomenon, for, truth be told, the Movement was going around in circles.

But going around in circles at a surprisingly high speed. Our days were twenty-seven hours long, lengthened by pure magic. Sixty-two-minute hours, and minutes that lasted forever. Manuel told me during one of those nights of insomnia that he had driven a van over to Biological Sciences at the IPN to deliver the *Gaceta Universitaria* (University Gazette), and that in the forty-two minutes he had spent there (after twenty years I still remember that he was there for exactly forty-two minutes— what better evidence of magic could you ask for?), he had fallen in love with eleven girls. And he described them all, one by one: a beauty mark on the neck of one, blue fishnet stockings, a green velvet hair ribbon, a very short lab coat, a pair of legs, two of them, fabulous legs . . .

I remember that I used to go home to our house in Roma Sur only occasionally, mainly to eat properly and engage in anguished conversations with my father, who fervently supported the Movement but thoroughly expected one day soon to have his son's corpse delivered to the front door. I would change my socks frantically, wrenching them from my feet, take a bath three times in a single evening, stow a couple of books in my sheepskin jacket, stuff my pockets with sugar lumps, and leave home dying with fright. I would walk as fast as I could to get to Insurgentes and find a truck that would get me closer to the University and my other home, where my fear would vanish once I was among my comrades. You couldn't reach the Ciudad Universitaria by bus, since public transport was curtailed. Street lighting was also nonexistent for the last couple of kilometers. So you had to rely on the underground railroad of hitched rides, on car-assisted solidarity to get you to the promised land. Arrival was frightening, too, because the University was under surveillance by secret-police patrols out on the prowl. The nights were getting longer now, and the days much shorter.

I remember Eligio Calderón and Adriana Corona eternally cloistered in the printing room with a couple of well-oiled and efficient mimeograph machines that produced thousands of fliers per hour. There they rediscovered Taylorism and the assembly-line rhythm of a Swiss watch factory. I remember how one day José González Sierra decided to extend a gallon of red paint with a gallon of white (which we didn't generally use for painting on walls) and ended up with a horrible pink that sparked a mutiny among the *brigadistas,* who refused to work with such shit. I remember Venadero squinting from lack of sleep as he glossed the first volume of Karl Marx's *Capital* for

Gloria Astiz. I remember Héctor Gama up on the school roof enjoying the sun and singing Mexican folk songs as he painted a message visible only from the helicopters. I remember my best street rally, opposite the Bank of Mexico: I had climbed up a lamppost and kept my balance thanks to the chaste hand of Maricarmen Fernández, the unchallenged leader of the brigades from Sciences, whose firm grip on my ass was the only thing that kept me from falling. I remember how we led the invasion of the Azcapotzalco market and the interminable applause of the women who sold vegetables there. I remember the day they let us into the streetcar and trolley-bus repair shops, and we painted up about a hundred of them in four hours.

I could never say it as well as Monsiváis: "Days without sleep, unforgettable dreams."

Throwing Corncobs

August was on the way out. Some high points. There were festivals. There were the challenges issued to parliamentary deputies to take part in a public debate, which the most wimpish of them declined because they were scared to come to the university. The first attempts to get a dialogue started, initiated by the government, were pettifogging proposals for negotiation that were swiftly aborted by the insistence on "public dialogue." The destruction of the statue of Miguel Alemán and the appearance in its place of a transient mural painted on the side of the metal casket containing his remains. Rallying for the liberation of a policeman who had denounced the corruption of his superiors. The discovery of a hundred or so keys in a strongbox belonging to the administration and our surprise at this, considering that during a month of occupation we had never needed a single key. A memorable sentence found in one of the books I had in my bag, a novel by Thornton Wilder, to the effect that anybody, once having lived, has lived an unbroken succession of unique situations. The rallies in San Juanico, the discovery of poverty-stricken neighborhoods, labyrinths of half-naked children, wasted pet canaries in reed cages, and standing water in the courtyards.

And, finally, the demonstration of 27 August, which started out from the Museum of Anthropology, filling the streets with the half-million that we were. It no longer mattered if the Movement was defeated, if they killed us all, and scattered our ashes across the Gulf of Mexico; this moment, now, was forever.

When the torches began to be lit that day in Mexico City's main square, the Zócalo, we still did not know how to weep. Unhappily for us, our delusions of victory were far too strong. The proposals approved at the last rally, namely, that students mount a permanent guard at the Zócalo and that there be a public dialogue on the day of the president's yearly speech to the nation, were a reflection (as justified as they were) of our inflated idea of our power. We were demanding unconditional surrender from the Mexican state. When the rally was over, a subdemonstration of three or four thousand people set off toward the "Black Palace" of Lecumberri, the jail where the political prisoners were held. We approached the prison and marched around it with torches flaring, yelling out to the prisoners inside, "We're going to get you out!" The jail was in darkness; we could see only the silhouettes of policemen high on the towers with their guns outlined against the sky. Someone hurled an old corncob at one of the guards, and he stepped back out of sight. Oddly enough, it never occurred to us to storm the jail. Many years later someone told me that our shouts were clearly heard in the cells.

Memo to Amnesiacs on How to Dent the Armor of a Tank with a Metal Pipe

Hours later that night the government counterattacked. Armored vehicles emerged from the gates of the National Palace, and soldiers with bayonets fixed advanced upon the three thousand students who had stayed to guard the Zócalo. Heroism at that time was closely akin to madness, as witness David Cortés, "El Ruso," who picked up a piece of metal pipe from the ground and went to meet one of the approaching light tanks. He was soon face to face with the fucking thing, which kept on roaring toward him. The soldier on top, manning a machine gun, and David locked eyes in a staring match. Suddenly, David leaped forward and began raining blows with his pipe on the tank's carapace, as though he really thought he could dent it. The tank came to a halt. We got our guy out of there, we had to drag him away, and the soldier never took his eyes off him for a second. Naturally, David lost all memory of this crazy moment. He asked us to tell him what happened, laughing sardonically. "Do I look like an idiot to you?" he wanted to know. "The kind of guy that would do shit like that?"

The clearing of the protesters from the Zócalo was not a rout, but a glorious withdrawal in which the armored vehicles pressed forward and the students fell back little by little, conceding ten or fifteen meters, slowing down, waiting until they almost touched the bayonets of the front rank of infantrymen. Things went on like this, block by block, as far as the Paseo de la Reforma, with car horns sounding in the night. And thousands of faces of residents in pajamas and nightdresses disappeared at their windows: witnesses to national history in the making. As the retreat proceeded, the protesters would stop from time to time to hold meetings for the sole benefit of the occasional night stroller. And so we went, street by street, each of us resisting the temptation to turn and run, backing up but never turning our backs on the soldiers, and singing. If heroism was defined by the capacity to stand firm in face of one's own fear, then . . .

The government's justifications for that night's action initiated a long catalog of cheap lies that still provoked derision years later. We were accused of ringing the cathedral bells, of insulting the national flag, of profaning the gates of the palace. They were lying like crazy. The eagle on the flag, which captures the serpent and accuses it of taking bribes, was smiling at us. We were true Mexicans now; and they, for the first time, even if they did occupy the presidential palace, were less Mexican than we were.

The next morning a rally of civil-service employees was organized in the Zócalo; the authorities obliged the workers to file out of their offices in strict order. These proceedings did not sit well with the bureaucrats, many of whom began shouting, "We are being carted about like sheep by Díaz Ordaz!" A few student brigades infiltrated the rally, and in the end the army had to be called in again to break things up. For the second time in twenty-four hours armored vehicles rumbled across the flagstones of Mexico City's main square. The little tanks buzzed madly through the Zócalo like bumper cars at a fair.

The streets were beginning to close. *Brigadistas* were arrested, schools were fired on. Yet the wave of mobilization was not slowing. Groups of workers started showing up at the schools, and workers' committees for solidarity with the students started to form. The first of these were in the semipublic sector: oil refining, railroads, electricity. There were not many, barely a few hundred. Massive flash rallies were held. Sometimes the police intervened to break them up, more often they arrived too late. City buses could no longer be used by the brigades—the risk of arrest was too great. On the other hand, the number of schools on strike across the country increased as classes began in other states of the Republic.

On 1 September, in his annual message to the nation, Díaz Ordaz pooh-poohed the Movement's demands and threatened to use the armed forces. At some point in his speech he apparently mentioned the navy. The next day a Movement leaflet, distributed citywide, petitioned the authorities to keep submarines out of the lake in the Bosque de Chapultepec.

Topilejo

Then came Topilejo. An accident in which a bus toppled down an embankment on the road to Cuernavaca and killed a whole lot of locals, it mobilized the small village, whose inhabitants demanded compensation for the injured and for the families of the dead, and the building of a hospital. The accident had enraged the community, and students went out there to organize, to extract restitution from the bus company, and to back up these desperate villagers living by the Cuernavaca exit ramp. The movement thus brought to Topilejo the students' experience with grassroots democracy, mobilization, brigades, direct action and . . . the commandeering of buses.

Toño Vera told me the story over and over, convinced that I didn't believe him. Next to him, nodding vigorously in agreement, was his faithful friend and comrade, a kid from Economics known as "Filemón, the Meek Guerilla."

Refinery- and electrical-workers' committees in solidarity with the Movement were emerging, small groups of a couple of dozen activists. In working-class sections of the city the first underground organizing committees were likewise coming into being. Was it conceivable that the Movement might expand beyond ourselves? Brigades from the more radical schools began searching for more aggressive forms of agitprop. Vans full of activists descended on the General Motors plant, singing and handing out leaflets, entering the inner courtyards in defiance of the security guards. The workers looked at us with a mixture of sympathy and bemusement, reminding me of how people used to look at Mister Ed the Talking Horse on television.

But still, the propaganda drive in the factories continued to grow. The brigades pressed forward, exploring the industrial areas, finding out what time the factories let out, and identifying those who, judging by the way they accepted a leaflet or stopped to listen to a speaker, might be future allies, possible friends.

Absolutely No Telephoning

The government refused to engage in a dialogue on the students' terms. They wanted nothing to do with a public dialogue, only secret negotiations in which there would be absolutely no loss of governmental prestige and absolutely nothing legal, just the same old trickery, empty talk, and opacity. For our part, crazy as we were, we demanded transparency. The only transparency on offer was the clarity of their repressive measures. The right wing of the Movement sought to retreat; the rector of the University called for a return to classes. This proposal was rejected massively in the assemblies. As each school voted against the proposal to end the strike, its students marched to the esplanade of the Ciudad Universitaria to announce their decision.

Handbills with a crossed-out telephone and bearing the message "This is not public dialogue" closed the door on the idea of secret negotiations, which we considered a trap. What happened next? The days were long, and many things happened. But liaison was their job now, not ours. Every day the street rallies multiplied, every day the propaganda brigades grew in number.

With La Quinta in Parque Hundido

We had set up an underground group with comrades from here and there—just to keep our hand in and not lose our old activist reflexes. We used cigarette brand names for pseudonyms: one guy was Lark, another De Prado, another Camel. Arlette, since she was Paco Quinto's girlfriend, was called simply "La Quinta." She was a girl from Tabasco with an arsenal of the crudest insults I had ever heard in those days.

Arlette and I planned to meet one day in Parque Hundido to pay a visit to a friend of ours, the son of a stationery-store owner, who had offered to help us steal 150,000 sheets of paper from his father's shop. When I spotted Arlette in the distance I started to shake. The park was full of riot police, at least two companies of the blue bastards, complete with rifles and grenade launchers. Some of them were lying on the grass, killing time; others loafed around on the sidewalk. They made you think of Capone footsoldiers, bored stiff as always from the waiting. The government had posted them here to close off Insurgentes to the north—heaven knew why, because no demos were planned, and anyway the brigades could easily slip through the holes in their net whenever they wanted to. Likewise there could have been *brigadistas* just two blocks away, holding a rally in Veiga, and those blue apes would have been none the wiser.

But I wasn't trembling on account of the riot police, I was trembling because Arlette, the irresponsible idiot, had come dressed in a cute little outfit, a miniskirt and white jacket, and here she was coming along on the same side of the street as the police, happy as anything and eating a mango on a stick. She walked past the first trio of them, provoking remarks that I couldn't hear from across the street, though I could see rapist written all over the guys' faces. She walked through a knot of about fifteen of them fiddling with their rifles. Was it just obliviousness, or had she decided to taunt them, to show them, true to some secret pact with herself, that she wasn't afraid of a bunch of goons? As for me, I could feel my hair turning white from fear. In those days violence would erupt in the most unpredictable ways, and the riot police were on edge, considering the forty-eight-hour stints, days on end without sleep, confrontations with students, and absurd advice from their commanders. Take, for example, the words of one who was overheard telling his men, just before they got out of a truck in front of the Poli: "These are Communists; they want to take the Virgin of Guadalupe away from Mexico." These footsoldiers were frightened—infected by their superiors, and their superiors by their own superiors. As always, you fear what you know well or what you know nothing about at all.

La Quinta passed among the riot police without looking at them, or, for all I know, she looked daggers at them, her eyes flashing like cut glass and sending shivers down their spines. I saw her go on for another ten meters before one of the men left the group and came up behind her, grabbing her backside with his free hand—the one that wasn't clasping his Mauser. Arlette wheeled around and swiped the guy across the face with her mango. The man staggered. I closed my eyes. I could hear nothing from so far away. I counted to ten, then opened my eyes again. Arlette was crossing the street, looking around for me. I didn't dare raise my arm to greet her. When she got to me, wiping the last traces of mango from her hands with a Kleenex, she said she was sorry for being ten minutes late. We didn't so much as mention what had happened. Everyone had their own madness back then. And if there was one thing we respected, it was everyone's own particular madness.

The Sound of Marching Feet

We were still fighting, but we had returned to the markers of reality. The euphoria of mid-August had given way to a stubborn resistance that was growing in all of us. The Movement still had many assets to deploy, much strength in reserve. Despite the pressure, the immense activity of the brigades continued: a massive propaganda effort, thousands of walls painted night after night, growing contacts with the population of Mexico City, the slow process of learning a lost language in which we could converse with the rest of the people. Every day more troops were moved within the city. Every day mass action became more difficult, but there were still ways to pull it off: the surprise convergence of different action brigades on a factory or commercial area, flash demonstrations, and the blocking of streets by four brigades acting in unison to create a mass rally. New sectors, or at least their vanguard elements, contacted the

Movement: primary-school teachers, general-hospital doctors.
A strange kind of warfare pitted the mobilized repressive forces
against the operational agility and speed of their opponents.
Our losses amounted to fifty or so people arrested per day. More
than half were released after being treated to threats, rebukes,
and sometimes blows; the rest joined the ever-growing mass of
political prisoners, prey to beatings and torture. On the other
hand, the enemy was quite unable to prevent the two or three
thousand rallies held daily. On 13 September the Movement
erupted onto the streets once more in a demonstration that left
its mark forever on the wet asphalt of Mexico City's streets. This
was the Great Silent Demonstration.

I remember the rain, and I remember the faces of the
demonstrators, their mouths sealed with insulating tape or
bandages to show that the silence was their choice, not one
imposed by the enemy. That, whichever way you cut it, our
power was beyond words. I confess that I had been utterly
opposed to a silent demonstration; the idea had come from the
center, which at that time was leading the Movement, and
besides, in those years I had no grasp of the power of spectacle.
I remember the succession of silent countenances but also the
eloquence of the gestures, the V-for-victory sign flashed over
and over again, the raised fists outside the United States
embassy, and the cheering from the endless wall of support
along the route provided by parents, by onlookers, by what at
the time was referred to as the people, protecting the flanks of

the march for kilometer after kilometer. I remember faces. Unforgettable expressions among the Preparatory 8 contingent. I also remember that I was thoroughly despondent that day, haunted by a broken love affair. I strove to combine my sadness and the silent joy around me into a single feeling. I was sad, but proud to be part of this multitude whose silence was only accentuated by the sound of marching feet. We had taken over the street, a street that led to other places, to points of no return, to the end of the world.

On 15 September we celebrated by throwing a big party in the Ciudad Universitaria. Paloma reminds me how different the national anthem sounded that night from when we had been made to sing it in primary school. We ate tacos and *sopes*, we tossed confetti-filled balloons, we danced with fifty-year-old ladies we didn't know, the mothers of Preparatory 7 comrades, and we drank punch to our heart's content. Heberto Castillo felt his role as master of ceremonies entitled him to marry a few hotheads, thus anticipating reality by a few months but earning himself more jail time down the line.

The next day all the schools voted once again on whether to continue the strike; not one voted against it. We kept up the pressure despite the approach of the Olympic Games, but you could sense that the government's final onslaught was coming soon. A few mimeograph machines were spirited out of the Ciudad Universitaria; our night patrols increased—as did our moments of panic; we organized a replacement coordinating committee designed to take over the control and organization of the brigades in the event of a repressive attack; we began holding some meetings in private houses off campus; we placed Movement archives in secure storage; and in the assemblies (with trembling voices, much nervousness, and not a little naïveté) we discussed our options in the face of repression. We expected the blow, but we did not know how brutal it would be.

Wherein We Learn That the Tanks Have Arrived

In memory, we tend to associate individuals with a single moment in the past. In memory, René Cabrera is not the enigmatic anthropologist of today but the first to call for a general strike in Zapotec, while Juan Gabriel Moreno is not an excellent mime but the prodigious driver of a Renault that made it from the IPN's Santo Tomás campus to the Ciudad Universitaria in thirty-seven minutes. Paco Pérez Arce is not the economist who later wrote a thesis proposing that cows be fed sugarcane so that they would give malted milk (thus foreshadowing the novelist he is today), but the guy who suggested distributing leaflets by means of miniparachutes. And Héctor Gama is not the journalist and photographer we know now but the man who saw the tanks.

From the roof of the café at Political Sciences, Héctor, better known as "El Chilito," saw the tanks arrive. To him belongs the small glory of being the first student of Political Sciences to see a tank on the lawn of the University esplanade. From the Philosophy Department, the loudspeakers were transmitting a poem by León Felipe, and we could hear it from where we were. Héctor started shouting, and even though I heard what he said, I did not believe it. I shouted back at him to quit his bullshit, and as he yelled, his face grew red. Then I heard the sound of the motors. We hurtled out onto Avenida Copilco. Romeo stopped to help a sister with a skirt so short she couldn't decently climb over the fence. Suddenly, from behind him came the sound of a weapon being pumped and loaded. Wordlessly, a soldier was pointing his gun at him. I slipped down the wall and off into the night down Copilco, along with Marco, one of the best Go players in the country. The girl in the miniskirt was an infiltrator; Romeo pulled two years of prison time.

El Chilito made it out. A few hours later we were in his house in Contreras printing up leaflets. I don't remember now whether it was then or a year later that the sound of the machine was accompanied by the barking of the dogs on the hill and the cries of his recently born daughter.

In Which the Virtues of the National Anthem Are Rediscovered

There were many who couldn't get out. They were trapped on the esplanade or in classrooms where they had gathered. The army moved through the University with bayonets fixed. Some of the soldiers broke windows with their rifle butts. They wrecked laboratories in Chemistry and projection rooms in Architecture. They hauled down the Mexican flag, which had been at half-mast. They were bringing those arrested to the esplanade and making them kneel down in a big group on the grass, when suddenly this mass of people threatened by rifles began to sing the national anthem: "*Mexicanos al grito de guerra . . .*" (Mexicans at the cry of battle . . .) Some of the students got to their feet and flashed the two-fingered V-for-victory sign. When exactly did the student movement recuperate this most worn-out of symbols? And when exactly did it appropriate that obligatory, rhetorical song, with Bocanegra's pompous lyrics and Nuñó's rhythmical air? If the anthem was ours, and it surely was, then who were they? Who were these foreign-born invaders? Years later I wondered what those soldiers must have felt. I knew what we felt, both those who managed to get away and those who were captured: a mixture of fear, rage, and impotence. They had deployed ten thousand troops to arrest six hundred unarmed students. It was the eighteenth of September.

In the next few days the Movement responded to this extraordinary attack. The National Strike Council continued to meet in Zacatenco, and the brigades continued their actions despite the arrests. Many massive rallies were called, organized by the school assemblies, but most of them were broken up by the police. Vocational 7 was assaulted by the riot police, but the students responded with Molotov cocktails; the Colegio de México was fired upon; and the police shot at various Poli schools in Zacatenco. Magically, brigade activity was kept up. I remember that the brigade committee had installed a portable mimeograph machine in the trunk of a car belonging to the daughter of a Distrito Federal functionary. The car would come to someone's garage, where stencils and paper had been readied and where flyers would be printed and left for pick-up soon after by a brigade; the car would then set off for another house, where the process would be repeated. We were living under the continual threat of arrest.

Coordination with the brigades from Philosophy collapsed when the police busted our contact in Coyoacán—just because of the way he looked.

Fanny and the Cop

I couldn't tell her that he was a cop, because how could you tell your girlfriend, who had just finished informing you that she had fallen for someone else, that that someone else was a cop— definitely a cop? You would sound pathetic, cowardly—like some asshole starting false rumors. But I could swear that the guy really was a cop and that the meetings held in a Chinese café with preparatory kids, who had once been offered arms there, were a lousy set-up planned by this tall skinny rat, a sup- posed preparatory student—at twenty-five—who had popped up out of nowhere as a second-rank student leader. I was also sure the guy was a cop because his left-wing talk never came out right. He wasn't like the new recruits, who had a whole battery of recently acquired ideas, all mixed up with ethical notions gleaned from the films of Pedro Infante. No, this guy talked in a way that seemed right but wasn't, because to an educated ear there was just something false about his language. His quotations from Mao or Che were correct enough, but this overgrown kid had never read Nickolai Ostrovsky, never even heard of Pavel Korchagin, was unaware that Marx had a thing with his housekeeper, and couldn't make cracks about ice axes or puns on the titles of Lenin's works. It was something like that—but more complicated. He was okay, but then again he wasn't, and besides, his final look, at the end of a conversation, was always an evasive one, devoid of the affection we all felt for one another at that time. And he was vehement in a way that never managed to convince me he was for real. I thought for a time that all the bad vibes were coming from me, not from him, and that if I hated the guy with such a distilled hatred, it must be because he was stealing my girlfriend and breaking up a relationship that, however tormented, was certainly a product of the times.

Anyway, she told me that she was in love with the guy, and it was all I could do not to blurt out that he was a cop, that she should watch out—and then, like the good Cyrano, I went off to weep in dark corners of the University. But I was no Cyrano, I was just an ugly little mouse, like the one in the children's book. After a time I left the university and began to follow my rival at a distance; one day went by, then another, until the day came when I saw him meeting with some creeps who eventually got into an unmarked police car with its telltale little radio antenna. So he *was* a cop, and I was so sure of it now that I convinced Regina to keep Fanny home the next time she was supposed to meet him. And that was when the committees of Preparatories 1 and 2 were arrested and jailed, at a meeting in a Chinese café where they had gone to get guns.

Nabbed

I was picked up in a police sweep one night after leaving Mario Nuñez and Elisa Ramírez's house to get some cigarettes. A patrol car stopped me two blocks from Calle de la Campana. No questions—just "Stop!" and into the car I went. Your appearance was a crime in those days; your youth, likewise. To be young was to be the enemy. They had a point. They took me to the Mixcoac police station. After a short wait my turn came. The agent of the public prosecutor was waiting behind a writing desk on a little platform. On my arrival a cop had taken my name down on a slip of paper—the first name, in any event, that came into my head—and the slip had been placed on the agent's table. He was eating a ham roll with a lot of avocado on it, and he used the paper to wipe his fingers. I hesitated.

"May I go out and look for her somewhere else?"

"Look for who?" he replied without looking at me.

"My sister. She hasn't come home."

He didn't answer. I walked out of the place between two policemen standing guard at the door with ancient Mausers. I'll never forget that they had their bayonets fixed. Those fucking bayonets were gleaming in the light of the moon and the mercury lamps. That's how I remember it, I swear. I got back to Mario's house three hours later—with no cigarettes. Everyone said how much they loved me and hugged me even though I had never got the smokes. They had already written me off.

By this time they were not just arresting brigades, they were shooting at them, and they still couldn't stop us. A group from Psychology tossed fliers from rooftops when baseball games let out at the Social Security Diamond in Cuauhtémoc. We would stuff the restrooms of office buildings with leaflets. We were still holding flash rallies at factory gates. Brigades met in the most unlikely places. Once I arrived with mine at a waiting room in the Tangassi funeral parlor, only to find that there were already two other brigades (unmistakable because of their appearance) meeting there and mingling with the mourning family members. Without even knowing it, we were developing tender feelings for other people's dead.

The Ginza by Night

At night your hands would sweat. No one was sleeping at their own place. We were waiting for the start of door-to-door raids to capture all strike-committee members. I had taken refuge in a hideaway belonging to the brother of Paco Abardía, a 2-by-1.5-meter room in Cuauhtémoc where this guy, known as "El Polvorón," used to take women he picked up. There were no windows, just a bed, and a poster on the wall that obsessed me: a Japanese travel poster showing the lights of Tokyo and captioned "The Ginza by Night." The Ginza pursues me to this day, it comes back to me even after all these years from that wall, from that room where, alone, I felt nothing but fear.

Those were times when I did not sleep.

Mimeographs

If the days prior to the army's invasion of the University had been all about the future, those that followed it were all about the present. We were trying to resist, to plan for the next two or three hours, to keep acting at all costs. After renewed combat, Vocational 7 fell into the hands of the military. The response was a massive rally at the Tlatelolco housing project. The National Strike Council continued to operate, maintaining a minimum of coordination. The brigades and the assemblies in those schools that had not yet been taken did the rest. On 24 September the army blasted its way into the Santo Tomás campus, home of half the Polytechnic schools. For the first time there was return fire: among the students defending the campus, no more than a dozen were armed with pistols and perhaps four or five with shotguns—but still, there was return fire. The riot police wreaked a bloody revenge on their prisoners, beating and torturing them. There were thirty wounded. This was just the prologue, of course, a terrible foretaste of what was to come.

We were beginning to live with blame. Who had died for you? as Retamar asked. Who had they arrested because you made a mistake about a meeting place? Why hadn't you been in Biological Sciences when the shooting started? What the fuck were you doing asleep while the riot police were attacking Vocational 7? Why, for Christ's sake, hadn't you been arrested? Survival plus guilt: a poisonous cocktail for the months ahead. All the same, the Movement was not yet defeated, indeed it was still showing signs of life on every side. Suddenly, as you were crossing Insurgentes, a slogan-bedizened bus would cruise right by you, or brigades would appear out of the blue, broadcasting their message of denunciation before fading back into the city. As survivors, however, we were becoming older, angrier, and more alone. We knew that a commission of the National Strike Council was negotiating, but the assemblies were being dissolved, and some schools were being abandoned even before they were taken by the army or police: their courtyards would be left empty, and the last one to leave would turn off the mains and padlock the door. The students were in retreat, organizing solely as propaganda brigades. The nights were the worst. Contacts lost, people failing to show at meeting places, and hours without sleep.

I met with with a woman who was coordinator of one of the department's brigades, which distributed propaganda printed with a mimeograph machine miraculously saved from the forces of repression. The machine was hidden in the bedroom closet of an actress whose husband was unaware that printing went on in his house in the mornings. She told me enthusiastically how they would conceal their leaflets in brown-paper bags from the bakery, covering them up with bread-rolls. The next day I lost touch with her. Her brigade had been fired on outside the Alameda movie theater.

One day "Doc" waited for me in his neatly pressed white lab coat, smoking behind the wheel of a green Volkswagen. We were supposed to go and retrieve a mimeograph from the house of Salvador, "El Indio," who had been arrested the day before. We were taking a chance. El Indio knew that if he gave up his address, they would find the machine and throw him into Lecumberri to rot. He would wait for us to get it out of there and would take the interrogations in the meantime. It was nighttime. Silently, Doc drove us to a lonely street. I think Salvador's place was on Narvarte. We drove past it twice; we saw nothing out of the ordinary. Doc and I were not friends—we had once fallen in love with the same woman. But that night, as I looked at his face in the shadows with the cigarette, I knew that he would have sooner died in agony from appendicitis than leave me in the lurch, that my back would never be so well covered, that my own mother would not protect me as well. Without saying so, we both knew that we could not allow either of us to be caught. We tossed a coin to see which of us would go into the house. We had a key. I won the toss, but then Doc said that it would be smarter to go in together—that if we were really going to load up the damn car, two would be better than one. He parked in front of the house and we got out. There was barely any light in the street. We let ourselves into Salvador's place, which was on a low floor. The mimeograph was in the maid's room. We packed papers and official documents into a shopping bag, tidied up, and filled a couple of cardboard boxes with Mao and Che books, along with a photo of Salvador in the Plaza de la Revolución in Havana, love letters he sent to his wife, and his old passport. We went back out. I carried the mimeograph while Doc hefted the two boxes and gripped the handles of the shopping bag between his teeth. We looked like a circus act. I was opening the door of the Volkswagen when a car with its lights off appeared at the end of the block. I shouted, but Doc had already spotted it, dropped the boxes on the ground, and produced a ridiculously tiny pistol from his white coat. The car without lights braked and someone shouted, "Don't shoot, man, it's Ana!" And we saw a girl get out of the car, also white-coated, but without a pistol. Another night volunteer for recuperating errant mimeo machines. Doc lowered his pistol and gestured to her to move the car. He was sweating.

"Hey, don't drop that shit on the ground!" he said to me, pointing to the mimeograph, a brand-new Gestetner. I made no reply—I was far too busy trying to control my trembling hands.

He dropped me off at the statue of the angel on Reforma. We

did not want one another to know where we were sleeping. We made two rendezvous for the next twenty-four hours. Doc went to stash the mimeograph in a private pediatric hospital. Ana followed him at a distance, to make sure he wasn't taken in, and then let the Medical School committee know that the machine, which we had named Sitting Bull in honor of El Indio, was in service once again. I walked down Reforma at two in the morning, slipped into Cuauhtémoc, returned to my little room, and closed the door. My hands were shaking, my teeth chattering. I was so afraid that my lower back hurt. I began to cry as I looked at the poster of the Ginza by night.

Dying a Little

I don't remember why we had to go to Preparatory 8 that night. Nor do I remember who was in the brigade. All I know is that the school was empty when we crossed the courtyard and that we were chasing shadows until we reached the auditorium.

I don't remember where the dozen or so drunken *porristas* came from and why we were unable to give them the slip. All I remember is how one of them had a bayonet and how he placed its tip against my stomach in a playful way, but then not so playful, and he cut me. All I remember is how one of my comrades struck his arm with a black umbrella that had a bamboo handle, and we ran out of there. I recall the umbrella very well. Also my bloody shirt and the bandage on my stomach, covering my belly button. And a pain that still comes back sometimes in my lower back, a pain that I recognize as the pain of fear: a sharp, shooting pain that recurs and leaves me covered in sweat.

Was this dying? No, because in those days there were others who were dying for real.

As much as I try, I cannot recall the features of that drunken *porrista* who played at killing me a little.

Even Liars Know the Truth

On 30 September the army relinquished the University buildings it had taken over. The government was hoping that the
Movement had learned its lesson and would call off the strike.
But on the first day of October the assemblies voted to hold out
and demanded that the IPN schools be handed back. The
Movement had tremendous resilience. In two months it had
created thousands of cadres, thousands of speakers. No sooner
did it find a space where it could act than it expanded into it,
built up its strength, reorganized itself, and once more set about
the tasks of deployment and propaganda.

On 2 October the army attacked the rally in Tlatelolco.
What happened is well known. The story of the massacre has
been told and retold. The attempt to falsify history—which the
machinery of the government launched moments after the first
students fell, hit by gunfire—demanded a response. The

response is in the second part of Elena Poniatowska's book *La Noche de Tlatelolco* (published in English as *Massacre in Mexico*) and in the thousands of Tlatelolco poems. Preserved there forever is the rebuttal to the false version of the facts offered by General Crisóforo Monzón, who said in an official statement that the army had intervened to restore order in the midst of an exchange of fire among students. The truth is there, as compared with the official version propagated by the Senate commission, in which the students are said to have fired first. Today everybody knows that the provocateurs were soldiers disguised as civilians, each wearing a single identifying white glove, soldiers from the Olimpia Battalion. Today everybody knows that flares thrown from a military helicopter were the signal to open fire, the signal for the army to begin to shoot into the unarmed crowd. Today even the liars know the truth. But there is little consolation in the fact that the version of the survivors has finally triumphed over the official story.

Everyone Blames Themselves—Forever

I arrived in Madrid at dawn on 2 October. I bought a newspaper on Castellana. An enormous photograph showed the soldiers shooting in Tlatelolco. I lost my voice. Hysterical mutism, the doctor called it. The doctor didn't understand that the Movement had struck me dumb as a punishment. I was not entitled to speak, because I had not been there, with the living and with the dead.

For years I blamed my father for getting me out of Mexico. I blamed myself for giving in to his insistence, to the information he had obtained that the Ministry of the Interior had an enormous file on me. And I blamed the fear I felt at the time about being a foreigner. For years I blamed my father, myself, anyone. Not to have been at Tlatelolco was much worse than being there and not dying. Eventually, though, I stopped blaming the old man: his common sense had very likely saved my life. The fault was not his, but mine. Nor is it any use saying that I was only nineteen. That was no excuse. Indeed, being nineteen was the very reason I should have stayed. Your task, if you choose to accept it (as they say on *Mission Impossible*), was to say no, and I didn't. To stay, and I didn't stay. Although I returned. I left Madrid after two days and returned to the department.

Tlatelolco Is Everything—The Rest Is Nothing

Over time, regrettably, the second of October, with the tremendous power of our four hundred dead, many of them nameless corpses tossed from military airplanes into the Gulf of Mexico that same night, with the images of the wounded being dragged off by their hair, captured for posterity by the camera, with the memory of blood on the wet ground, with our retinas invaded and forever marked by the light of the two flares that started the massacre, with the stories of hospitals assailed by judicial-police officials intent on finishing off the wounded—regrettably, that day has been isolated.

In memory, the second of October has replaced the hundred days of the strike. The black magic of the cult of defeat and of the dead has reduced '68 to Tlatelolco alone. Perhaps because I was not there, because I perceived the events of the Plaza de las Tres Culturas through the accounts of Santiago Flores, who was shot in the leg, through the silence of the candles and flowers placed on the ground there on the second of November, a month afterward, and through the eyes of the myriad anonymous narrators—perhaps because of this I managed to escape the curse. The rest was the Movement. And it continued.

It Is Made Clear That Barricades, Once Built, Lodge Immediately in Memory

The massacre terrorized parents and drove their children crazy. It put us on the defensive for the first time. This time, it was for real. The Movement's leadership—cadres formed over the last four years of student struggle, natural leaders thrust into the streets by the insurrection of '68—was decimated. At this time a couple of thousand students were imprisoned. Those among the better-known figures—a handful—who had managed to survive the massive arrests at Ciudad Universitaria, the attack on the Santo Tomás campus and on Zacatenco, who had not been caught on 2 October, had not been wounded or killed, either went into exile or took up forms of clandestine action that isolated them from their student base. The bloodletting, in short, was immense, and the less politically sturdy sectors retreated to a waiting posture. Ten or twelve thousand diehards strove to keep the Movement alive by means of information-brigade work, rallies that put the speakers' lives at risk, and press conferences at the Casa del Lago in the Bosque de Chapultepec. In effect, a truce was imposed that was to last until the Olympic Games were over.

What was that time like for those who were not locked up? We knew that at Military Camp 1 the arrested had been tortured, that our comrades, our leaders, our friends, those with whom we had shared a floor to sleep on or a last bite of food or a cigarette, had been mauled, punched, terrorized with blank ammunition, clubbed, held down under the filthy water of the horse troughs, castrated. . .

Infiltrators and snitches had been freed. News of tortures filtered out continually through a network of fear, thanks above all to lawyers and relatives. Fantastical confessions concerning the origin and nature of the Movement had been extorted from a number of our leaders; most had proved impossible to break down. These were all *our* prisoners, inseparably and absolutely bound up in our lives. That they were inside and we outside was pure chance. Just as they were inside for us, keeping a prison bed warm for us, as it were, we were likewise struggling to deal with their absence by keeping their places on the bench for them. Between those inside and those outside was an ocean of love affairs, comradeship, fraternity, guilt, and sacrosanct loyalty. We may have been only 17, 19, 20, or 25 years old, but we felt a terrible responsibility, we bore a truly loathsome weight on our shoulders.

In late October, the three demands were framed that would focus our efforts over the next month: unconditional freedom for the prisoners, return of the schools, and an end to repression. The government handed the schools back, hoping that the students would back down. But during the first days of November the schools, assembly by assembly, obstinately voted yet again to continue the strike. We were not going back to class without our prisoners.

Leaving—and Staying

We were sleeping in my room at the family house in Roma: René Cabrera, the finest poet of my generation, the one who had written "We do not need to say we are growing closer to grow further apart"; Jonathán Molinet, better known at Preparatory 1 as "El Hombre Lobo"; and me. We took turns sleeping. One of the three was always at the window, watching the street and ready to raise the alarm. We had a rooftop escape route half-planned in case they came for us in the middle of the night. The other two slept. René and I used to talk in our sleep. El Hombre Lobo claimed that we babbled incoherently, that when one of us said something in his sleep the other would answer. I am sure he was right. The days weren't long enough to tell one another all the stories we had to tell. Terrible stories—stories of persecution, more arrests, tortures. I fancy we were all talking in our dreams during that November.

I gave my blue plaid sheepskin jacket to Mario Nuñez and saw him off as he went into exile with Marcelino Perelló and Guillermo Fernández, student leaders among the most wanted by the police. They had escaped by pure luck. I had nowhere to go, and I didn't appear to be of any great interest to the law. I had already left once.

So I kept watch one night out of three, with El Hombre Lobo and René. Waiting for the black cars with their antennas, but they never came.

The Dead

Lourdes lived in the area behind the airport. She was a serious girl, snooty even, but tragic, blessed with the rare self-awareness that takes it for granted that life is bound to abuse you. We had been comrades in preparatory school. Through other people she got in touch with me at the house where I was hiding. A cryptic message: she would be in the third row of the Cine París, second show. I don't recall the film. Nor do I have a clear memory of Lourdes's features. She had curly hair and seemed to belong to another generation, to another period, a 1950s-type woman. Years later she joined a guerilla group and was disappeared. At the movie she leaned close and whispered in my ear: "I have photos of the dead."

It was very dangerous to know things. "The dead" were the people murdered in Tlatelolco, the bodies that had vanished. We set up a second meeting. I said I would get a group of foreign journalists together. Lourdes left the movie theater ahead of me. I didn't ask her how she had got the photos; I assumed she had sneaked with a camera into the military airport behind her house. The rumor was that an airplane had left the night of 2 October and that the bodies had been flung into the Gulf of Mexico. Murder was not enough: the bodies had to be disappeared also.

Two days later I waited for Lourdes at the Monumento de la Madre beneath a sun with *cojones*—distinctly un-Aristotelian, as Alejandro Zendejas, another of our poets, would say. Lourdes never made it. They had arrested her.

Ending But No Happy

The resistance lasted one more month. Hundreds of rallies, debates, brigade activity. . . But we were in the stage of no return. We needed to find new forms of struggle, and we couldn't. In the end, on 4 December, the last schools accepted the resumption of classes. I voted to end the strike, thinking that we had to bring the repression to an end and reorganize. The National Strike Council disbanded. Everyone swore in their own particular way that there could be no forgetting, that something would have to be done, that one day we would return.

In forty years' worth of memories, I can recall no greater desolation than the one we faced the day classes resumed. The flowerbeds were trampled, no one had cigarettes, precious few smiles were exchanged. We returned to defeat, with the prisoners and the dead wandering through the courtyards like ghosts from *The Communist Manifesto:* sons of the Revolution of 1848,

German Jews adrift in Europe, Poles with no fatherland—and these eighteen-year-old Mexicans in search of the country glimpsed during those few days and now fading. I didn't last long: studying was quite meaningless. After trying to strangle a sociology teacher who made fun of the Movement on the first day of class, I quit school.

One day I fainted halfway through a meeting. Then I also quit the political organization in which I was active. I got married. The marriage lasted four months. Fanny walked out. I let the kitchen things grow moldy, and I wrote a novel that was turned down by four publishers. To cut down on laundry I stopped wearing socks and underpants. I spent my nights awake, sitting on the floor in a bedroom with a carpet but no furniture. I felt I had lost so many things, but I couldn't define them. I found a repellent job as a scriptwriter for soap operas. I combined it with an equally horrible job writing horoscopes for a television program, and a third, a night job, writing radio stories for drivers. I decided I needed urgently to return to two things: my country and my life. I started looking for a way back.

In Which We Return to the Idea of Ghosts and Their Persistence in Time

When all was said and done, it had been nothing but a student movement lasting one hundred and twenty-three days. No more and no less. Yet it had given us—given a whole generation of students—a past and a country, a ground beneath our feet. In the ensuing months thousands of us, within the University and without, tried to find our way. The most unhinged joined an urban guerilla struggle that over the next five years bled out into a mercilous dirty war. A very large group of us went into the neighborhoods and founded community organizations that for twenty years offered a model of popular resistance. Others went into the factories in search of the reasons the student movement had not resonated with the workers. Others again sought to transform higher education, starting unions and pushing for educational reform. Still others ended up in the countryside—an even stranger land. On these disparate journeys we took with us all our strengths and all our weaknesses: a voluntarism inured against defeats, an ingrained stubbornness, a lot of book-learned Marxism, a lot of sectarianism of the old and the new varieties, and a lot of fucking ignorance. There were distinct virtues in the mix: a notion of politics as moral, which would take a few years to develop fully, and a healthy feeling that we were not immortal.

Twenty years after, a fair number of those of us from back then are still alive and kicking. Others wore themselves out, many were corrupted. Most did not pile up more defeats in life than those that were imposed upon them. Of course there were defeats, a shitload of them, but surrender was rare. Sixty-eight bequeathed us the reserves of defiance and determination that had been the motor of the Movement as a whole, and it infused us with a sense of place, a firmly rooted feeling of nationality.

We ran into each other again in 1973, at the time of the doomed attempt to defend Chile, and again during the unrelenting call for pro-Nicaragua solidarity in the seventies; we saw each other in the days of the earthquake and during the University Student Council (CEU) movement in 1986. In reality we saw each other continually: at the time of the electricians' movement; during the Spicer strike; at the La Pascual cooperative and during the marches for Demetrio Vallejo; during the upheaval at Social Sciences, when we wrought disaster by trying to transform the universities but merely turning them into centers of a Neanderthal Marxism; when architecture students were building sheet-metal houses in Santo Domingo; in the transformation of the Mexican press; when a movement of socially conscious doctors arose and a crazy generation of honest labor lawyers; in the tenants' legal struggles; in the revival of critical social commentary; when people were fired for refusing forced PRI membership in 1985; on street corners; during lonely nights cursing at the television; in the courts as we went through our divorces; on the garment workers' marches; in the registry-office ledgers when we baptized our sons Ernesto; and during so many poisonous benders as we made it to forty and found ourselves bewildered—genuinely surprised—to be growing older. We saw each other, too, in the launching and destruction of dreams and projects and in the books we read. And we met again at the elections just past.

And so we go on, bearing with us the ghosts of our dead, the ghosts of our occasional traitors, the ghosts of our suicides. There are nights when I see Dulce María chewing on her pencil and Carlos Thierry falling asleep on his chair and Doctor Lino Osegueda smiling at me during the Spicer strike as if we were invincible, as if we were immortal, as if he wasn't going to kill himself two years later.

And I cannot let go of Alejandro Licona's toothy smile, even if Elisa Ramírez tells me that he disappeared in the south of France, that he may well have drowned at sea or be locked up under a false name in a mental hospital. I still say to Licona,

"We're going to keep on giving them hell, aren't we, Alex, my old buddy?"

But then there are days when I see myself, and I don't recognize myself. Bad times, when the night prolongs a rainy day, when sleep won't come, and I wrestle vainly with the computer keyboard. I realize then that we seem doomed to be ghosts of '68. Well, what's so bad about that? I ask myself: better to be Draculas of resistance than PRI-ist monsters of Frankenstein, or of modernity. And then the keys produce graceless sparks, weak flares, memories that are sometimes painful but most of the time raise a slight smile; and I long for that old spirit of laughter; I mourn, growing fearful of the dark, for an intensity now lost, for that feeling of immortality, for that other me of that never-ending year.

TWO EPILOGUES

I. Twenty-Five Years After (1993)

In early August 1993 we dinosaurs began being summoned by word of mouth, telephone calls, and a brief announcement in the press to a reunion at a meeting place of our own choosing. Dinosaurs (whatever Spielberg may think) are history-loving little beggars, nostalgic, recalcitrant to authority—all of which explains why their favored grazing area turned out to lie in the past and specifically in the auditorium that they themselves, one glorious afternoon twenty-five years earlier, in the thick of the '68 Movement, had renamed "Che Guevara Auditorium."

So I headed down to the south of the Distrito Federal, something that is harder and harder for me to do, because I wanted to see how time had treated the '68 old guard. And also because the invitation had given the venue its proper name—*our* name—as opposed to the archaic "Justa Sierra Auditorium"

(Sierra being a bureaucrat of the Porfirio Diáz era, quite distasteful to me).

The idea was to take a look at us, and at me, in the light of the twenty-five years gone by since the Movement of '68, that mythical origin of almost all of us, indeed of almost everything.

Memories of that time were always coming back: tender, incisive, sometimes rough-edged, caustic. What made these confounded fantoms so durable?

I can easily explain how they affect me. This flotsam was, after all, morally formative in my case, so much so that even on bad days I can summon up a host of discrete images: David Cortés taking on a tank with his length of pipe, the bulging eyes of Héctor, "El Chilito," when he spotted armored vehicles trundling across the esplanade of the Ciudad Universitaria, the menu at Political Sciences under occupation, and some very private feelings of fear. But what about the others? Were they moved merely by a nostalgia with its back firmly turned on present-day reality?

That our ghosts had staying power could not be doubted: when the day of the meeting came, that vast University auditorium was packed, half of it with forty-something Movement veterans, the other half with eighteen-year-olds. Nor were all the dinosaurs red, and here and there a pterodactyl could be seen—even a variety with the less than heroic pedigree of a PRI-ist vulture.

From this throng emerged an ill-defined organization that declared itself open to all who cared to join: the "Twenty-Five-Years-After Committee," known thereafter (to economize on letters) as Com25. That evening Com25 called for two initiatives: first, the institution of a "Truth Commission" to cast light on everything concealed by the official accounts of the '68 Movement; and secondly, the initiation of a petition to the government to open up all its archives. These actions would conclude with the publication of a manifesto on 4 December, the anniversary of the day in 1968 when the general student strike was abandoned.

I decided that night to join these efforts. The novel and the screenplay I was working on would just have to wait.

Three hypotheses: (a) a myth is not necessarily a lie, (b) generally speaking, the myth is the rumor-borne truth of those that got screwed (after all, the victors control national television, and (c) myths do not aways embody the finest aspects of the story— sometimes they preserve only the cheapest and most ridiculous details.

The legend of the wanderings of the Aztecs as they searched for their home on the lake; the quest for the nonexistent Aztlán; Wyatt Earp at the O.K. Corral; the romantic heroes of the poems of Byron or Espronceda; the exploits of all the big-hearted outlaws (Robin Hood, Dick Turpin, Chucho El Roto); the day Dad stood up to his boss and told him to go fuck himself; songs in which three horsemen appear in the heavens (God, Zapata, Jaramillo); Pedro Infante, troubadour champion of the poor. . . Such elements are the raw material of mythology—not lies, but something else, something essential: the stuff of our own lives.

Of course, there is also Benito Juárez as the "little pastor" of the nation, the claim that Elvis Presley was born in Sinaloa, Uncle Joe Stalin visible through a lighted window in the Kremlin working away late into the night for the fatherland, the fucked-up vision of the essential Mexico proposed in Octavio Paz's *The Labyrinth of Solitude,* the on-screen machismo of Rock Hudson—all the makings of myths that are perfectly silly, not to say idiotic.

Despite the paucity of attempts to tell the story—a couple of fiction films, a couple of documentaries, two or three novels— awareness of the '68 Movement had been growing over the last few years, nourished by the vague stories parents told their children, the nostalgic memories of the glory days recounted by a generation since trapped by years of vain struggles and month after month of shit work, of lurching from one financial crisis to the next, of juggling principles with the need to survive.

Myth material par excellence.

Demythification is not the only option, however. Another is remythification.

In response to the mobilization of '68 veterans, a host of seekers after the "objective" truth about the Movement emerged in the media. Dubbed "objectivity hounds" by us dinosaurs (as everyone knows, dinosaurs are basically herbivorous and passionate), what they were after was a digestible version of the facts that would in no way upset the present of the yuppies of Ali Baba and his forty (PRI-ist) thieves. The "objective" version of '68 would surely be aired in public in all its certitude, then duly vanish from the popular middle-class imagination.

They would say things like, "It was only a student movement. You also have to see things from the State's point of view. What did they think—that it wouldn't defend itself?" Or, "Things are different now. Remember, there has been a great deal of progress in the last few years."

For myself I think, on the contrary, that if there is something from '68 to be defended, it is its long-lived magical aura, created with love and persistence, in a country of cheaters and cheated, by dint of real democracy tenaciously practiced for 123 days (or 130, according to Marcelino Perelló, who is always correcting my simple-minded statistics) of university occupations and assemblies at all levels.

Against the digestible account of the objectivity hounds, I recommend the counterversions of Miguel Hernández ("the inextinguishable ray") and Michael Ende ("unending history"), which for decades now have energized thousands of Mexicans in their ongoing struggle for full democratic rights.

I am thus in favor of the fantasy, the antiauthoritarian myth of the Movement, along with the accompanying bloody-mindedness with which that Movement fought for democracy. I am in favor of saying it yet again: It is not over yet. As for objectivity, I don't give a royal shit about objectivity.

Because, when you get down to it, this is a myth that gives them a major pain in the ass.

I was at the first meeting of the Twenty-Five-Years-After Committee. We often met in bookstore cafés, and people at nearby tables would crane their necks to glimpse this reemergence of the dinosaurs. With enormous pleasure I rediscovered faces from back then, a crowd I love: Adriana Corona, Gastón Martínez, Blanquita, Trobamala, Eugenia, García Mota, Filemón, Carlos López. They were better looking now, improved even, rumors to the contrary notwithstanding; at the very least they had a more finished aspect, with their opulent mustaches, unabashed silver locks, and reading glasses. So many defeats had somehow not been in vain. My generation, if nothing else, had achieved a certain style. Born to lose but not to bullshit, whispered the phrasemaking gnome in my head.

In '68, looking back, we dressed a bit like timid customers of clothing chains like Milano and El Niño Elegante. What could be more horrible and puritanical than those wide-sleeved shirts and slightly flared pants! Now, though, we looked like a bunch of unemployed anthropologists, our attire ranging from jackets with leather patches at the elbows (like Dustin Hoffman in *All the President's Men*) to turtleneck sweaters (the young Jean-Paul

Belmondo). On the other hand, the complete disappearance of miniskirts among my female peers took some getting used to.

Our meetings tended to follow a pre-set ritual: photos of Movement days were passed around, films were shown, and we chewed over old history for all the world as though we had not lived through it, as though we needed to convince ourselves that it had all really happened.

One of the many Com25 meetings, held in a university auditorium with students and political groups in attendance, almost ended in a brawl. How naïve it was to suppose that all this was a thing of the past—that the sectarianism of the old left had vanished along with the old left itself. Far from it! The sad fact of the phenomenon's staying power was only too plain to see. Manifestly, tyrannosauruses—flesh-eating predators as opposed to us herbivorous dinosaurs—were quite capable of reproducing, and thereby perpetuating, a contagion that drives its victims mad, turning them into the mortal enemies not of the real agent of their poverty and suffering (the oh-so-far-off repressive State) but of their closest neighbors, with whom differences must be invented as quickly as possible so as to inflame hatred against them.

On the domesticated television show *Nexos*, Rolando Cordera tried to wring self-criticism from a few stubborn defenders of the '68 Movement. "So, did something go awry?" he persisted.

"Was there a failure of organization? Was something not working properly?"

And I thought to myself, yes, without a doubt—and from the outset. But I also thought, just like the television panelists, that I wouldn't be the one to say so. The fact is that seeing the downside is a burdensome luxury that the defeated do not tend to indulge in public.

Who were the real inheritors of the Movement of '68? The University Student Council movement of the late eighties clearly had an incontestable claim to the mantle. But it was important not to exclude the democratic syndicalism of the 1970s; the Cardenista electoral revolt; the brigades of volunteers who transformed Mexico City as they worked amid the devastation of the earthquake of 1985; the workers' cooperative of La Pascual; the critical journalists fired over and over again by their papers; or the people's lawyers who went to Nicaragua and in many cases left much of their souls there. Even a significant number of those who took part in the Cardenas anti-PRI revolt of 1988 could claim to be true heirs of '68. Obviously, therefore, the veterans of the '68 Movement, thousands of them now in their forties and firmly ensconced in the middle and professional classes, had simply no monopoly on '68 as their own little baby.

Us and the others: in a passageway I heard a bunch of kids claiming that '68 was something to do with other people, because they themselves were not even born back then. To me this seemed like historical illiteracy. I wasn't around when Hidalgo tolled the bell that started Mexico's struggle for independence, but that doesn't make me distant, foreign, or without a viewpoint in that regard. It is not a matter of having been there when others were not. Not about other generations having better myths than one's own. It is all about entering into conversation with Jules Vallès and the Paris Communards, with Flores Magón and John Reed, or with Juana the Oaxaqueña who, in Cuautla with Morelos's army in 1812, lifted her dress and bared her ass to the *gachupines*—the Spaniards in their firing positions opposite—to make them waste ammunition.

The trouble was that official versions, fully copyrighted, were seemingly under construction, and it was precisely these versions that needed to be destroyed. The Movement was entitled to more than the accounts offered by its participants; it also deserved the versions of its inheritors. Property rights to '68 belong also to those who were not yet born at the time.

Throughout that September, as demonstrations and other events were being organized and many interviews and documents related to '68 were being published, I kept hearing the same phrase at meetings, rallies, on television programs, radio broadcasts, and even in private conversations: "The Movement does not belong to anybody." Yet most of the time I got the impression that what was really being said was just the opposite. Experience has sensitized us to doublespeak, and in these voices I couldn't help hearing the whispered message that the Movement of '68 was indeed the private property of the speaker.

The term *botear*—meaning to pass around a can to collect money—was born in '68. And here we were, "canning" once more, at the intersection of Mexico City's Eje Central and Avenida Juárez, in the shadow of the Latin American Tower. Once more we were poorer than church mice, because Com25 had proved particularly adept at running up bills (due mainly to the cost of announcements of its activities in the papers). The result was really quite entertaining. There were about twenty of us. Flash sociological analysis: the forty-something professionals were working much better with the eighteen-to-twenty-year-olds. Smiles all around.

The area we were in was blighted by unemployment. "I'm cold," someone said. On balance, said someone else, the main thing wasn't the money—the main thing was being back in the street. Sound the bugles!

That night I listened with Paloma to Raúl Jardón's program on educational radio: "The '68 Movement in Memory." An impressive effort that got the whole family gathered around the radio—shades of the 1950s. We liked the way Eberguenyi narrated the week's events. We liked Jardón's selection of period music, reviving Donovan and Leonard Cohen, Dylan and Oscar Chávez. We liked the old voices singing, *"Cuando todo granadero sepa leer y escribir"* (When every riot policeman can read and write).

The seriousness of the program was much enhanced by the main interview with Marcelino Perelló, unquestionably one of the most lucid voices of the '68 generation. He called for two things: the renewal of the Movement's demand for public dialogue—the initiation, in other words, of that impossibility, a Mexican glasnost, something the country's authoritarian government could never conceivably grant—and a return to everything in the Movement that had been revolutionary or profoundly transformative in character.

The Truth Commission came into being in a tiny theater packed with press. Its members included some of the best known writers, lawyers, journalists, and actors in Mexico: Alonso Aguilar, Sergio Aguayo, René Avilés, Bernardo Batiz, Jorge Castañeda, Felipe Ehrenberg, Luis Javier Garrido, Miguel Angel Granados Chapa, Hernán Lara Zavala, Froylán López Narváez, Sara Lovera, Lorenzo Meyer, Héctor Ortega, Elena Poniatowska, Javier Wimer, Eraclio Zepeda, José Agustín, Carlos Monsiváis, and Carlos Montemayor.

The purpose was not only to learn more about the events of 1968, but also to make the facts public.

Com25 bequeathed six issues to the Truth Commission for its consideration:

1. Clarification of the charge against the Movement that it was the outcome of a plot or conspiracy.
2. Origins and motives of the repressive action of July 1968.
3. Genesis and unfolding of the events of 2 October 1968 and the identification of those responsible.
4. Clarification of the contradictory information released concerning those killed and wounded during the '68 Movement.
5. Legitimacy of the penal judgments passed as part of the repression of the Movement.
6. Definitive assignment of responsibility for these events.

It fell to me to work alongside Ilán Semo as Technical Secretary to the Commission. For several months witnesses would be interviewed and documents examined. Commission meetings, held on the upper floor of El Juglar bookstore in the south of Mexico City, brought together Movement veterans, ex-soldiers, and neighbors and relatives of the dead. Letters were received, too, from former government functionaries and former police officers.

In due course a very long report was published which established that the Movement's prime causes were social in nature and that the State's response consisted of repression, censorship of the media, and lies. A list of the names of the victims of the Tlatelolco massacre was drawn up, and evidence was laid out showing that it was a sector of the army, under the control of the President of the Republic, that coordinated the shooting in Tlatelolco.

Luis Tomás Cervantes Cabeza de Vaca had a moment of glory during a press conference, when a Televisa reporter challenged him, none too graciously, as follows: "You were one of the ones who elected the Truth Commission. Who, might I ask, elected you?"

"I was elected," came the reply, "in July 1968 by a student assembly at the University of Chapingo, and, as far as I know, my mandate has not yet been revoked. All the comrades on the Twenty-Five-Years-After Committee were duly elected by their school assemblies. . . ."

Thunderous applause.

Another apt rejoinder was that of "El Pino" Martínez de la Roca, delivered with the half-bitter smile that suits him so well, in response to a question from a young woman reporter from Channel Eleven who was interviewing him, and clearly enjoying it, so that the generation gap between the two was bridged by the force of emotion: "It certainly isn't the most important thing," he said, "but I sure would like someone to tell me why they kept me in jail for two years, six months, and five days."

I now made friends that I had never made in '68, doubtless for lack of time. One was Cabeza de Vaca, once a student leader at

Chapingo; another was Salvador Ruiz Villegas, sometime leader at the School of Engineering. My friend Paco Pérez Arce says that meeting someone you haven't seen in twenty years can leave you with a sense of loss, but in 1993 I had the opposite experience, for throughout those days I had a strange feeling of reconnection.

The two above-mentioned characters were a tad crazy—crazier than most, in fact. After our meetings they would walk all the way home—supposedly to clear their heads. Late one night I found myself trotting beside them through San José Insurgentes, then through Nápoles. As we went past the big houses, trying not to step in dog shit, we decided the best thing of all was to have discovered that having different opinions was no sin. That there is more than one path to Rome, that left-wing thinking is ultimately ethical in character, and that who knew where Rome would turn out to be anyway? The sort of spiel, in short, that might well have been heard twenty-five years earlier.

When, a good while ago now, I wrote the pages that precede this epilogue, my main concern was to solidify my own memories. Now, in 1993, as I revisited those memories I looked at them once again to see whether the bath of nostalgia into which I had plunged over the last few days really had anything to do with them. I discovered that memories not originally mine were now becoming part of my own narrative, that the lived and the told, the heard and the seen, were fusing in my mind. Memory was being collectivized, and others' memories were becoming part and parcel of my own.

On 2 October 1993 we were in the street again. Even though the slogan I proposed—"One day of glory for so many days of shit"— was rejected in favor of the far more traditional "Today, like yester-day, for democratic rights," I was still pleased. I was in my Sunday best. I had brought both my most loving memories and my abiding hates back into the street.

For endless kilometers—so endless that we took to chanting "*The Three Musketeers* is not the same as *Twenty Years After*"—I marched alongside Paloma and my daughter. I was not the only one: a good many comrades had brought their kids. A surprising demonstration, really, with parents and kids together, vying with one another to see who could come up with the best chants, who could dream up the most really unreal country.

II. Thirty-Five Years After (2003)

Every time someone declares it forgotten, transcended, resolved, or dead and buried, it comes back. The '68 Movement is just plain ornery that way.

In the June 2000 elections the PRI fell for the second time: the thousand-year Reich of the cattle-thieves was disintegrating. With this rout of the PRI, our generation had at last fulfilled its pact with the devil: its vow to get the PRI out of Los Pinos, the presidential residence.

This is not the place to characterize the decaffeinated transition that has since taken place. An encounter did occur, nevertheless, with thousands of the absent: social pressure obliged the Vicente Fox administration to set up a special public prosecutor's office to address the political crimes of the 1960s and 1970s, the so-called dirty war.

Over the last ten years the persistence of the intellectual

community and of a number of newspapers and magazines has repeatedly turned the spotlight back onto the '68 Movement and the question of who was responsible for its repression. Photographs and films have been dug out of archives, an excellent documentary has been made by Carlos Mendoza, the files of General García Barragán have been opened, and a book published, *Parte de Guerra II,* with a commentary by Carlos Monsiváis and Julio Scherer García that sheds much light on the role of the army. Carlos Montemayor has made a semitechnical study of the Tlatelolco killings that even manages—on the basis of the positions of the military sharpshooters and the trajectories of their fire—to demonstrate that the Presidential guard fired on both infantry and students. Special issues of the magazine *Proceso* published long-concealed photographs of the torture perpetrated in police stations.

Very few doubts remain as to the facts. What had already been clearly grasped by public opinion is now solidly documented.

However, as long as the murderers are not brought to justice, the wounds will fester. The special prosecutor's office has moved only under external pressure, lurching this way and that, opening investigations and calling on ex-presidents to testify, which they refuse to do. As for us, obdurate as ever, thirty-five years down the line, we are back in the street yet again.

Mexico City, late November 2003

PACO IGNACIO TAIBO II, author of more than fifty books, is a distinguished historian and essayist. He is also renowned world-wide for his detective novels. His numerous literary honors include two Dashiell Hammett prizes, a Planeta prize for the best historical novel, and the Bancarella Prize for his biography of Che Guevara.

DONALD NICHOLSON-SMITH has translated numerous works from the French and Spanish including Guy Debord's *The Society of the Spectacle* and Raoul Vaneigem's *The Revolution of Everyday Life.*